ADVANCE P

D1039554

"*Tom is the expert when it comes to being successful in real estate...Read and execute the ideas in this book and you'll be on your way to more success.*"

"*Simply the best actionable techniques for mastering the real estate market.*"

"*Tom's passion for creating a better real estate experience for all is evident in every chapter.*"

"*Easy to follow tips and techniques to break through barriers and achieve success.*"

"*Every agent should own and study this book! It will accelerate your success and enable you to make more money, in less time, with less stress!*"

TOM FERRY
PUBLISHING

MINDSET, MODEL AND MARKETING

The Proven Strategies to Transform and
Grow Your Real Estate Business

ISBN   978-1-5445-0040-9 *Hardcover*

978-1-5445-0041-6 *Paperback*

978-1-5445-0042-3 *Ebook*

MINDSET, MODEL AND MARKETING

MINDSET, MODEL AND MARKETING

THE PROVEN STRATEGIES TO TRANSFORM AND GROW YOUR REAL ESTATE BUSINESS

TOM FERRY

CONTENTS

INTRODUCTION

———

I wear a lab coat...After coaching real estate agents and teams for nearly thirty years, my team and I have studied and documented the art and science of success in real estate. Together we've helped countless agents better serve their customers while creating a life and a business they love.

One of my favorite ways to teach and share what I've learned with agents is through my popular series on YouTube called the #TomFerryShow. On my show, I've taken my research and the proven business-building techniques and strategies and put them in a fun and easy to watch lesson. In this book, I've taken the best of those strategies and research and put them in an easy to read guide you can start implementing in your business right away.

I've created this book with three sections in mind: Mindset, Modeling, and Marketing.

The book starts with the mindset section, because that is where success starts. One of my favorite sayings is "Your head is a scary place to be!" From my experience, you've got to have the mental toughness and growth mindset in place so you can more powerfully implement the proven strategies and techniques shared in this book.

Mental toughness is more than just a theory for me in my own life and business...On July 7, 2016, my wife was diagnosed with breast cancer. I, along with our boys, family, friends, and a terrific medical team, rallied and supported her to victory. We're so grateful to be on the other side of surgery and chemo. I've had to practice and continuously improve my mental toughness. Mental toughness is staying in inspired action despite the circumstances surrounding you.

After mindset strategies, I cover modeling. Consciously or not, all of us are modeling someone or something in our lives and our businesses. In this section, I share with you the systems, structure, processes, and skills that I've found to create the most success for your business and your life.

The last section is all about marketing. As the great Peter Drucker said, "All business is innovation and marketing." In this section, I share some of the best marketing methods I've seen work time and time again. I've also included some very effective scripts that you can use immediately.

What's possible for you? Are you thinking big enough? Know that I believe in you, and my desire is that this book will inspire you to do what you love, serve clients that you love, for the people you love. Now that's a great business!

As I mentioned earlier, my life and family have been impacted by breast cancer and this book is dedicated to my wife Kathy. Proceeds will benefit breast cancer research.

Remember, now more than ever your strategy matters and your passion rules!

TOM FERRY
FOUNDER AND CEO

ACKNOWLEDGMENTS

———

I'd like to thank all the real estate professionals who've watched, shared, and commented on the #TomFerry-Show! You are the reason I do it. Thank YOU!

And to my team, Taz, Dan, Dani, Sarah, Briana, Richard, John, Mark, and Marni, for making the show and this book come to life!

And to our business coaches and internal team for supporting by watching, sharing, and helping so many learn and implement the lessons.

And finally to my wife, Kathy, and my boys, Michael and Steven, I love you. Thank you for being my constant source of love and energy!

MiNDset

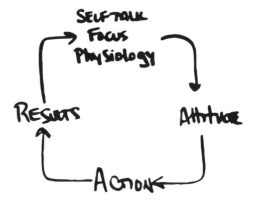

Working with thousands of agents from all over the world, here is what I know: agents either have a growth mindset or a fixed mindset. Agents with a growth mindset thrive and those with a fixed mindset struggle.

A growth mindset is about seeing problems as opportunities. When you've got a growth mindset you are setting the foundation for massive success. Your mindset is everything, and fuels your drive to keep going when things are difficult. When you commit to the actions and habits required to improve your mindset, you will be on the path to achieve the growth and success that you truly deserve.

TAKE CONTROL OF YOUR SELF-TALK

There is one thing that affects your mindset more than anything else...It's that voice inside your head! I'm sure you're thinking, "Tom you are crazy! You hear voices!?"

I'm not talking about those kinds of voices, but more like that dialogue that is running through your head almost constantly. We all experience this in varying degrees. Think about the last time you had to make that uncomfortable phone call with your customer because there was a problem...What did your self-talk look like?

"My customer is going to be so angry! They will reject me as an agent and tell their friends. Then I'll never sell a home again, and I'll starve!"

You know it's not that bad, but those voices can get really loud. That kind of self-talk isn't doing you any favors. Like anything else, you can easily improve your self-talk and psychology.

Check out the image on the previous page. My mentor Brian Tracy showed this to me years ago, and it is something that I think about on a daily basis.

It all starts with your self-talk, which leads into your attitude. This is a big deal because your attitude is essentially how you view the world.

From there it is all about your actions, and those come from your attitude. Actions get results, and depending on what kind of results you got, the whole process will start over.

My Son the Tennis Player

My son is a superstar tennis player (I may be a bit biased), and getting rid of negative self-talk before a match is crucial to the outcome of the match. So, before every match he repeats these powerful affirmations:

> I now command my conscious and unconscious mind to give me the skills to serve aces, be quick to the ball, play consistently, hit away from my opponent, and close out the match. I want this right now, right now, right now!

Feel free to create your own powerful affirmation and use my son's model if you need help. Affirmations or positive self-talk are a great way to remove negative thoughts and get your actions aligned with your goals.

Where Is Your Focus?

You've probably heard the quote, "What you focus on, expands." This is absolutely true! Shifting focus is a key technique for developing a positive attitude. Your attitude is based on how you view all situations. Say for example you're on a listing appointment and don't get the business, do you ask yourself, "Ugh! Why does this keep happening to me?"

What if instead you asked yourself, "What can I do

differently to earn the business I know I deserve?" If you ask yourself a better question you get a better answer! It's a small change in language that makes a powerful change in your attitude.

Physiology—The Way You Move Your Body

In addition to your affirmations and the things you focus on, there is one fast way to alter your self-talk. It simply involves changing your physiology.

I want you to try a quick experiment. Stand up, raise your hands in the air, look up, and smile as big as you can. How do you feel? Silly, OK sure, but notice how happy you feel. Deepak Chopra taught me that there's a connection between your body and your mind. If you move your body in a powerful way, it instantly impacts your attitude. Powerful postures give you a positive attitude, it's that simple!

DEVELOPING YOUR MINDSET

———

There are a ton of factors that most people think are essential for success in real estate. They think about sales training, a solid marketing plan, or even a rockstar team. All those things are incredibly important, but there is one thing you have to have to be successful in real estate...A growth mindset!

I'm constantly looking for ways to strengthen my mental resolve. Here are some of the things I'm doing every day to improve my mindset.

Start your morning right.

My morning routine is about twelve minutes long, but

yours could be longer or shorter depending on how much time you have.

I spend a few minutes breathing. Deep breaths that you can feel down in your stomach. I do this to calm myself, clear my mind, and get oxygen into the body.

While still maintaining those deep breaths, I spend some time being grateful. This is so important and scientific studies have shown that gratitude is one of the keys to being happier. I usually think of about five to ten things that I'm grateful for, and they don't always have to be big things. Sometimes I'm just thankful for a meal with my family or spending a few minutes outside on a nice day.

After that, while still breathing intentionally, I begin visualizing. I visualize health and vitality in my body and I visualize success for the top three goals that I have for the day.

Your body is a temple.

If you don't move it, you lose it! Get your body moving whether it's at the gym, outside, or in the comfort of your own home. My goal is to hit the gym a few times per week because I know it makes me feel better. Like I always say, when you feel good, you perform good!

Diet and hydration are super important too. I'm always making sure I drink enough water and eat a diet that is healthy. I've been eating a lot of sardines lately and really enjoy them!

I'm a coach, not a doctor! Be sure to check with your doctor before you make changes to your diet or exercise routine.

Feed your unconscious.

To quote Napoleon Hill: "Whatever the mind can conceive and believe, it can achieve!" If you feed your unconscious mind with negative thoughts, want to guess what will happen? What you feed the unconscious mind ultimately affects your actions and outcomes.

Instead feed your unconscious positivity. This positivity is generated from gratitude, the things you are taking in (books, media, news, etc.), and you will position yourself for success.

CLOSE THE LOOPS AND TAKE MASSIVE ACTION

———

When I look at people I see the amazing potential they have for growth! The life, dreams, and desires they are striving for are available to them! Here's the problem...

Your head is a scary place to be!

When most people are faced with a choice to take action, their subconscious kicks into overdrive. So for example, if I asked you to call five expired listings, you might think of all the awful things that could go wrong. What if they yell at you, or hang up, and then you start visualizing a whole list of awful things happening, ending with you not being able to work and feed your family!

Is that the reality? Of course not!

Here are some things you can do to break that pattern of thinking and be in the right frame of mind:

1. What am I holding onto that if I let go of I'd be free to create, grow, or have fun?

Every single one of us is holding on to a story that we think is true. These are the things that we have told ourselves to be true based on a few past negative experiences. We've let these experiences have a tremendous amount of power in our lives, but they shouldn't.

Don't let those past negative experiences become the story of your future events. I want you to change those stories and remove their power! How many of those open loops are still around in your life? It takes some work, but you can remove those patterns.

Altering those patterns starts with changing your mindset, and then visualizing success. It takes time and effort, but I believe in you and know that you have the power to achieve your full potential!

2. What "incompletes" are causing you to drag?

Incompletes are things that create uncertainty in your

business. It could be new marketing strategies, your database, prospecting, or anything else that causes uncertainty.

Like removing those limiting beliefs, you can handle the incompletes that are causing you to drag! It might mean learning those new marketing strategies (or hiring someone who does), creating a plan for prospecting, or simply getting a firm grasp on that daily number. (I talk about that later in the book.)

Don't be like the vast majority.

So when people are faced with these doubts and inconsistencies they start to hide. They chase distractions and focus on things that aren't the highest and best use of their time. When you have all the weight of those inconsistencies on your shoulders, you can see how it would prevent you from taking action.

If you want to be successful, you have to take action.

BE A LEVEL 10 WITH NO APOLOGIES

Right before I launched my previous book, *Life! By Design*, I hit an interesting crossroads. I was on the verge of breaking through my glass ceiling, and I was definitely outside my comfort zone.

Have you ever been there before? I was so close, but I set myself up for a little bit of self-sabotage. I was in my head, and I was scared about what was on the other side of success. In the middle of all that, I called my coach and here's what she told me.

"It's easy to be complacent and underperform your potential." It's easy because this is what everybody does. You have to be committed to live, work, and play at your best.

Too many times we set our standards lower to appease the people around us. When you start finding success, cynical comments usually follow. We all know that when you land that big listing, most people don't congratulate your hard work. They think maybe you found some shortcut or did something underhanded to get it.

Look at the Realities of the World We Live In

Most people don't act at a level 10 because they fear how everyone else will react around them. When you start to disrupt the status quo by being a 10, it affects the people around you.

I'm issuing a challenge: are you willing to be a level 10 in all areas of your life with no apologies?

I want you to be a level 10, and you can do that with these three steps.

1. Stop giving your power away.

The first thing you have to do is stop apologizing for having goals and dreams. Your drive and desire for success doesn't require an apology.

What that ultimately means is that you have to stop caring what everyone else thinks about your ambitions and desires to serve others and your family. When you get overly concerned with how others view you, you are giving your power away.

2. Be on your path; everyone else is on theirs.

We all have our own path to walk. You have to get rid of the mindset that if everyone else isn't operating at a 10, they are wrong, and you are right. They may just be at another place in their own journey, and there is nothing wrong with that.

When you encounter those friends, family, coworkers, and others who aren't operating at a level 10, make a small shift in the way you see them. Simply say, "I choose to operate up here. I love and respect wherever you choose to operate." No judgment; simply love them for who they are.

3. Put on your cape. #SuperYou

I want you to think big with me for a second. How would the superhero version of you act? What would you be like if you put on that superhero cape and got to work? What time would #SuperYou get up in the morning? How aggressive is #SuperYou in sales presentations?

Visualize that super version of you. See yourself wearing

that cape and performing at a level 10 in all areas of your life.

I already believe in the super version of you, but you have to believe it too. You must accept the fact that you are a winner and that you were born to do something special. You are meant to do something great! I know you are more than capable, and given the right actions and habits you can achieve the greatness you deserve.

Are you ready to be a level 10?

It takes work, but I know you are up to the challenge to be a level 10 in all areas of your life.

Where have you been less than a level 10?

I bet there are certain areas of your life where you are crushing it, but you and I both know there are some areas that could use some improvement. Maybe it is with your family, career, spirituality, health, or something else. Listen, I don't want you to beat yourself up if you aren't a level 10. This is a self-assessment to see where you can improve.

Some people see themselves at a level 5 or 6 in certain areas. For me the reality is a little bit different. I see myself as either a level 10 or a level 1; there is no middle ground.

My mindset is about making that full commitment to being a level 10, and halfway there isn't going to cut it.

Get clear on what a level 10 looks like in each area.

Like any goal you are striving to achieve, you need to have a clear picture of what a level 10 looks like. Don't have a clear picture? Think of how #SuperYou would perform and go from there.

Can you think of a model of someone who is living a level 10 in that specific area? Take a step and look at what they are doing to be successful. Like I talk about in the "Model" section of this book, subconsciously or not, we all have models. You might as well model your habits, behaviors, and strategies off someone who is crushing it!

Just pick two areas and attack!

I know some people reading this book will think about all the areas they need to work on and feel overwhelmed. If you're feeling overwhelmed, it just means that you are underplanned.

Don't get caught up in a bunch of areas that you want to improve! Instead just focus on one or two areas and go. We are all works in progress, and being a level 10 takes time.

Not sure where to start? Think about the areas of your life that are anchors—meaning that if you were free of this thing, you would dominate other areas. Simply start there and take action.

Get some help.

If you've been to one of my events or watched a few episodes of the "#TomFerryShow," you've heard me talk about working with a coach. I've had a coach since I first started working in sales about thirty years ago.

Having a coach really helped me achieve my full potential and take action when I was afraid. The coaches I've had over the years have provided accountability and given me the confidence to keep moving forward when times were tough.

I don't think I'd be where I am without the coaches I've had over the years. If you are looking to up your level of success, I'd highly recommend coaching. Whether it is from my company or another company that is specific to the industry you are looking to achieve success in, it will make the difference in what you can accomplish. If you want to learn more about my coaching programs, check out TomFerry.com.

BE YOUR BEST AT WHAT YOU DO BEST

———

How are you feeling today? Are you alive, excited, and full of energy? Whether it is my team at the office, or people I meet at events, I always get asked, "How do you maintain this incredible sense of energy and passion?"

What if I told you that passion and energy are a choice? They are like a muscle, and they need to be exercised every single day! You have to work on how you feel on the inside because that radiates to how you communicate with people on the outside.

I recently had this thought and I wanted to share it with you...

Do What You Love, with People You Love, for the People You Love

When you have figured those things out, you can line up your intentions, mindset, and actions. Because you know that when you feel good, you perform good! I want you to be at a place where your intentions and your behaviors become automatic. This is how you make your job feel like it is effortless.

I want to help you get more energy and passion in your life, and asking yourself these questions will help you get there!

1. What do I love about selling homes?

Seriously, what do you love about selling homes? Think about things like: the neighborhood, customers, transactions, and solving problems. When you have this figured out, the work you are doing becomes effortless because you're focusing on the things you love!

2. What do I love about my clients and prospects?

Don't just think about those clients who are difficult; take a big step back and think about what it is you truly love about your clients and prospects. For your clients, this might be helping them find a new home by being a counselor and guide. Or for your prospects, it could be as simple as meeting new people and helping them solve problems.

3. What do I really love about finding new clients?

Hopefully you didn't read that statement and think about the pain of cold calling, lead generation, and setting appointments. I'd encourage you to change your mindset to think about all the people you can impact and help! As a real estate agent, you have the potential to reach out to thousands of people over the course of your career. By the way, if you don't like finding new customers, you sure picked a strange business to be in!

4. Who am I honoring by doing my work?

If you really want to shift the perspective of the work you are doing, think of it in terms of who you will be honoring by being successful with your work. It could be based on religion, family, or simply a commitment that you have made with yourself to do your very best.

Suddenly the work you are doing on a daily basis, including those tasks that aren't always fun, take on a totally different meaning. If you're honoring someone with your work, I'm willing to bet that you won't see work as a chore.

5. Am I willing to make calls for the people I love?

This is a yes-or-no question: are you willing to have that hour of power and make phone calls for the people you love? Think about that question the next time you need to make calls, and you might be procrastinating a little bit...Are you willing to do the work?

Do what you love, with the people you love, for the people that you love.

OVERCOME YOUR EXCUSES

———

You know what you need to do. Maybe it's that one task you've been putting off doing, like finishing your marketing plan or putting that hour of power into your schedule to make sure it happens.

We've all been there. You set out to get that one painful task, but all sorts of excuses start popping up. Suddenly all these little things start feeling more important and you find yourself procrastinating with a long list of excuses of why you can't do that "thing" you've been putting off.

Common Excuses

While excuses come in different sizes and different shapes, chances are good you've faced some of the same excuses most agents out there have faced. Here are a few of the most common excuses I've seen in about thirty years of coaching successful agents:

1. "I can start tomorrow…"

You have to start right now and take massive action. That means even if you don't feel like doing the work, you can't wait until tomorrow. Because we both know that if you wait until tomorrow it probably won't get done.

2. "Not today; first I have to____."

We all have those things that we tell ourselves we have to do, but I'm talking about all those little things that feel way more important and fill up your schedule. If you have a plan and schedule in place, it helps you get clear on your priorities.

3. "My morning routine just isn't supporting me…"

Your daily routine is incredibly important! You have to align your behaviors with your goals. When your morning routine is filled with the important things (reading a good book, exercise, meditation, etc.), you are setting yourself up for the win. If your morning routine means hitting the snooze button one more time, you are going to have a tough day!

4. "My goals aren't up and visual…"

You need to have your goals up so that you can see them. If you have them up, this also means people in your office will hold you accountable. Your odds of follow through will go through the roof!

5. "I have too much on my plate right now…"

Everyone is busy. Seriously, we all have so much going on, and there is always something else that needs more time. Make sure that you have a clear goal in mind and prioritize your actions around achieving the goal.

The Mindset to Overcome Excuses

Let's be clear…The reason most agents aren't getting things done isn't because of scheduling or the excuses they tie to scheduling. Ultimately it is a mindset problem. A few tweaks to your mindset will make a huge difference in what you can get done and how you feel about doing it. Ask yourself these important questions…

1. What do I need to be doing more of?

Don't overthink this question, but take a step back and get clear on what you need to be doing more of. This might be following up with more clients, sending more marketing emails, or simply making a few more phone calls each day.

2. What do I need to be doing less of?

Most people tend to focus on what they should be doing, but fail to see where they are spending their time right now. I'm willing to bet if you went back through your schedule you'd see plenty of examples of things you should be doing less of.

You want to do less of the things that take up too much of your time or simply don't provide the results you are striving for. In the Model section of this book, I talk about how you should outsource tasks you're not good at, or even build a team to help you focus on the things that are the highest and best use of your time.

3. What habits do I need to start?

You can learn a lot about a person based on their habits. These are those actions that have become ingrained in us, the things we are often doing without even thinking!

Maybe it is the collection of habits I talk about in the Modeling section where you create a powerful morning routine. These are the habits that set your intentions and set you up for success.

What is one habit you could start tomorrow that would improve how you performed in your personal and your professional life?

4. What habits do I need to stop?

Are there a few habits you need to stop? It is super easy to get caught up in looking at your phone all the time. You know, that 24-7 email checking...Maybe it is constantly looking at Facebook, or simply being distracted with work when you should be present with your family.

It's Your Responsibility: Take Back Your Power

Like any change, fighting those excuses will take time to see some results. Understand this, when you take ownership of your excuses you are taking responsibility for your own actions. That means you aren't letting external circumstances, how the market is doing, or anything else get in the way of your success.

Make no mistake...When you give into excuses, you are letting them rob you of your power. When you are giving away that power, it becomes nearly impossible to reach that next level of success.

DON'T COMPLAIN ABOUT UNCERTAINTY

———

Do you know that agent who complains all the time? It might be the person you see in the mirror in the morning and who is also reading this book right now!

Like giving into excuses, when you give in to the habit of complaining, you are also giving away your power. Complaining sends a message to those around you, and I'm sure you can think of one or two complainers in your life! When you spend time with complainers, you see that they are energy sucking vampires!

Change Your Mindset

A change in an attitude and mindset is what is going to

make the difference. Here are a few tips to help you get the success that you know you deserve.

1. What got you here won't get you there.

This is one of my favorite sayings, because of how true it is! You and I both know that we can't follow the same actions and habits that have got us this far and expect them to give us even better results! What may have been a surefire thing for years won't be a guarantee today. You have to be constantly testing and measuring and looking for ways to improve.

2. Stop being positional.

So many agents get very positional about what works and what doesn't. Maybe they tried sending a mailer or running a Facebook ad and didn't quite get the results they were looking for. Now they have created a position forever for what works or doesn't based on just one experience!

There are certain tactics that will work better than others depending on the market, but it is up to you to investigate which strategies work best. I want you to have the growth mindset that allows you to try new ideas, ones that you know have already worked in the marketplace.

3. The market doesn't care what you are good at.

There are a ton of agents who have gotten really "good" at something over the years. Here's the problem: the market doesn't care what you're good at. In fact, if you were in real estate before the Internet was around, you know exactly what I'm talking about.

Real estate trends shift and markets change. Even though that happens, the market doesn't care what used to work for successful agents in the past!

Coaching

If you and I were having a coaching session right now, I'd want to share a few things with you so you don't get stuck in the three points noted previously.

1. Assess yourself.

Be honest about your psychology and its effect on your results. Take a step back and look at the bigger picture over the past few years. Which one of those three points hit closest to home? What kind of shifts in your mindset do you need to make to overcome them?

2. Assess your market.

No one knows your market better than you do. Assess your market and take a look at what customers are expecting from real estate agents like you. I know you've already experienced success in your market, because you are good at a number of things. Which things are you good at, and how can you get better?

3. Create a "my business in five years from now" plan.

What do the next five years look like for your business? This isn't just about numbers and GCI; I want you to dream up all the ways you are going to serve your customers and grow your business!

Five years from now, what do you think buyers and sellers will expect? What kind of agent will you need to be to help them find the solutions they need?

Don't just make this a mental exercise. Write down your ideas or have some place you can capture them to be reviewed and discussed later.

4. Start the new, while doing the old.

Although I'd encourage you to start some new things, that doesn't mean you should stop the things that have been working for you. If you have some strategies that have been working for years and are continuing to provide good results, keep doing them!

Remember that change is inevitable, and adding a few new methods on the way you grow your business will keep you sharp. Like I always say, make sure you are testing those new methods and looking for ways to make them better.

GOAL SETTING

What goals are you striving to achieve? Goals are such an important focus, and they start with having the right mindset. Most agents struggle with a fear of growth and limiting beliefs, and those in turn become their "default settings" for everything. That kind of negative mindset spills over into creating goals too.

Instead of living by default, I want you to live by design. This means shifting your mindset a little bit, and I know you'll be happy you did!

Set Big Sexy Goals

Seriously, I want you to think about big sexy goals. Don't limit yourself to incremental growth in today's market. For most agents that means they did $X last year and you want to do 20% more. With that kind of thinking the wave of opportunity is going to pass you by.

Instead, ask yourself these questions:

- What is my total addressable market?
- How many transactions are being done?
- How many homes are there?
- What is my goal?
- Do I want 1%, 5%, or 10% of the market?

Your goals have to be impactful! If you don't wake up in the morning emotionally charged about your goals, then you aren't thinking big enough!

Also remember that your big sexy goals can help you make decisions! Thinking about trying that new lead source or switching CRMs? Will it help you achieve your goals? Great, then do it! If not, let it go.

Overcome the Gap

You set this crazy intention, this exciting goal, and then something happens...Maybe you get stopped, run out of money, or can't figure out how to do Facebook ads.

I've been there too. If you get stuck, it means you have to

learn and grow. You have to figure it out and do whatever it takes.

Do you have that "whatever it takes" kind of mindset? Are you willing to work hard, provide more value to your customers, and commit to achieving those big sexy goals?

Be Flexible

Too often I watch people overly romanticize about doing the same thing over and over again because it used to work in the past. You've got to be a little agile and flexible. Maybe say to yourself, "Hey, I'm doing this, it's not working, let me make an adjustment."

This isn't a setback on achieving your big sexy goals; this is about making those adjustments so that you can succeed.

Believe You Can Succeed

I believe in you, and I know that you can absolutely achieve your goals. Do you believe in yourself? Do you have the mindset that will keep you going when things get tough? Can you visualize yourself achieving your goals? What will it look like when you succeed?

Don't be afraid of setting those big goals. Think bigger, and commit to success.

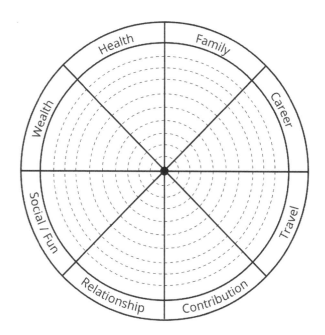

THE SECRET TO GETTING EVERYTHING YOU WANT

———

I love helping agents like you grow both personally and professionally. At several of my events, I've had agents take a look at the eight equities in their life. This is a powerful exercise that I would like to do with you right now.

Let's start by taking a look at the eight categories on the wheel:

- Family
- Career
- Travel
- Contribution
- Relationship
- Social/fun
- Wealth
- Health

Look back five years; where were you with all the key equities of your life? Draw a line. Now, look at where you are today. Have you improved? Where are the areas you can improve?

Then declare where you want to be in the next five years and give yourself three goals for each equity to build around for the next five years.

What's Your Vision for Five Years from Now?

Imagine the kind of life you want, and what it would look like five years from now. Picture the people you want to impact, and the things you want to do. See all the different areas of your life where you want to have an impact and write down one- or two-word phrases and then a series of goals behind those.

Do you really want to make that vision a reality? Share it with people you know will hold you accountable.

BEING BUSY DOESN'T CREATE INCOME

———

So many agents are stuck in that "busy" mindset. Being busy for the sake of busy sort of feels like work, but what's really getting accomplished? Is the work you are doing moving the needle and getting your business closer to accomplishing goals?

Most of the time "projects" don't create income. Think about it, would you call your bank and say, "Hey, look, this month I'm not making my mortgage payment; can I send you a sample of the projects I was working on instead?"

You have to have the mindset of doing what it takes to make sure the cash is coming in. On the surveys I've done with the thousands of coaching clients that are part of my ecosystem, I've seen some similarities. It takes about fifty conversations to equal one sale.

You know the game, whoever books the most appointments WINS! Preview appointments, listing appointments, a first buyer, first time initial meeting, showing appointments, or meeting with someone at Starbucks for fifteen or twenty minutes to talk about real estate could have a positive impact on your business. Knowing how important those appointments are, you have to schedule time to make the calls, do your follow-up, and plan out your next move.

DO WHAT MAKES YOUR HEART SING

———

Are you operating at an inspired level? Or are you tired, grinding away at work, and stuck in that "Eeyore" state of mind? You know what I'm talking about: that mopey, depressed, lack of energy agent...You can probably picture someone like that right now!

I want you to live life to the fullest and I can show you how to live at that inspired level. There is a formula that you can use to get the most out of your business and your life.

Here are three areas you need to have aligned to make that happen.

Life Ambitions

These are your passions and goals plus your time management.

1. What makes your heart sing?

These are the personal ambitions that fuel you to do the disciplined things in your business. This is more than just work you do on your business; these are things like hobbies too! Hobbies are a great thing, and they help provide balance from making your whole life about work.

Take some time and get really clear on those things that make your heart sing! What makes you happy? What are the types of challenges you enjoy conquering?

2. Schedule your year in advance.

Don't put off your passion and purpose just to do more work! There will always be work to do, and if your default mode is playing catch up, you won't ever make time for the stuff like vacations, events, family time, etc. The only way to ensure those things happen is to get them on your schedule well in advance. Think about what the next year looks like. Do you have those things scheduled in?

Business Plan

This is the plan you have in place for your business and the goals you will achieve.

1. What is the purpose of your business?

We exist because we know that the vast majority of real estate professionals underserve their consumers. It is easier to do the work not only when it touches just your head or your wallet, but when it touches your heart. You know that you are providing a service to your community and your customers. Think about this as more than just a "job" but as a way that you are helping people solve their problems and guiding them while they make one of the biggest financial decisions of their life!

2. What is the theme of your year?

Do you have a theme for the year? For example, I know an agent who uses the Journey song "Don't Stop Believing." By giving yourself a word or phrase you can emotionally attach yourself to, it gives you a boost and it is like putting on that superhero cape!

3. When are you going to complete your business plan?

One of my favorite sayings is "how much of what, by

when." You have to complete your business plan. These are your numbers, actions, and KPIs (key performance indicators) for your business.

Marketing That Acts as Fuel

Marketing is essentially the fuel for the engine that drives your life.

1. When are you going to complete your marketing plan?

You've got a marketing plan, right? One for the next 365 days that outlines your strategy and the methods you are going to use to grow your company.

If you don't have your marketing plan done yet, when's the deadline? I'm serious about this! Set a date and get it done. If you don't have a coach, find someone to hold you accountable to your date!

2. How are you going to track and measure?

If it matters, you have to measure it. Think about cost per leads, sales, etc. You might have heard me say, "Marketing is math!" Test and see what works best for you in your marketing across different channels. If you need some tips on how to create marketing that works, be sure to check out the marketing section of this book.

3. When is marketing in your schedule?

Do you have a time when you are regularly working on your marketing? This is the dedicated time you spend on doing the marketing. When I talked to my most successful clients, they outlined the ultimate daily routine:

- Forty-five minutes focused on marketing
- Fifteen to twenty minutes on role playing
- Ninety minutes for appointment setting and prospecting

Put marketing in your schedule and decide how much time you are going to spend on your marketing!

BE *EXTRA*ORDINARY

———

At the beginning of last year, I issued a very important challenge to the agents who are part of my coaching program. I asked them about the kind of business they wanted to have in the year going forward. Before I get to that question, I want you to take a look at your commitment to the following areas:

Morning Routines

How are you spending your mornings? What are the habits, routines, and activities you are spending time on? Are they positive things that are improving your mindset, or are they negative things like watching the news, spending too much time on social media, or sleeping in?

Hours of Power

Are you making those calls? Have you put time on your calendar every day for that hour of power? If you need more tips on how to make your hour of power more effective (or how to start doing an hour of power) check out the model section of this book.

Tracking Your Performance

The best way to know if you're successful or not is having a means to track your performance. It could be a graph, chart, or digital program, but there need to be some KPIs that you associate with your progress toward your goals.

Attitude and Mindset

How's your attitude today? Are you alive, excited, and full of energy? More importantly, are you committed to having a good attitude and the right mindset every day?

Follow-Up and Conversion

Anyone can get more leads, but you and I both know that the real money is made in conversions and follow-up. Have you been following up with your leads? Are you satisfied with your conversion rate?

Marketing

Is your marketing where it should be? Is it in line with your brand and providing value to your customers?

Listing Presentations

Are your listing presentations something you are proud of? Are you committed to improving them? Go to the marketing section for tips on how to improve your presentations.

Buyer Appointments

How many buyer appointments do you have scheduled? How could you add more buyer appointments to your schedule?

Team Meetings

Don't just look at the frequency of how often you meet with your team, but think about the quality of your team meetings. Does your team know "how much of what, by when" and is everyone on the same page for goals?

Role-Play Sessions

The last thing you want to do is practice on your customers!

Do you have people that you are role-playing scripts and dialogues with on a regular basis?

Business Networking

How is your network? Are you regularly attending events and connecting with the people in your community? Are you connecting with people outside your community to mastermind with?

The Question

Are you willing to take all those areas and go from ordinary to EXTRAordinary?

If you are committed to these things then I already know that you are not an *ordinary person*. The vast majority of the world is ordinary. Most people don't even notice the self-limiting beliefs and glass ceiling they have.

One my favorite sayings is "Routine is the sign of an ambitious individual." I know that just by looking at someone's routines, I can predict their future. That means if you have ordinary routines you'll have ordinary results! Don't complain about the ordinary results you get if you are just taking ordinary actions.

Five Letters

I want you to be EXTRAordinary and take EXTRAordinary actions! This is your chance to break out of the norm and do something amazing. It is the conscious choice to add those five letters to everything you do.

Looking at this list I just mentioned, can you think of a few of those areas where you can step up your commitment from ordinary to extraordinary? What would your business look like?

MODEL

Either consciously or not, you've been modeling your business and behavior after someone. We all do this; it's normal. Yet be careful who and what you choose to model. Why? Let me tell you a story:

An agent came up to me after one of my events and I could tell by the look on her face that something was going on. I wasn't sure why she was upset and she started crying. Even though she was dominating in her market, her personal life was incredibly stressful and things weren't going well at home. The woman she had been modeling her career after was in a completely different space...she was near the end of her career and her family was already grown. The woman I met at the event was following a flawed model that didn't serve her. It had brought her a ton of success professionally, yet it did not serve her personally.

Modeling is a very important aspect of your career and personal life. We all have models, and I encourage you to find the models that empower you toward the success that you deserve.

In this section, I'll show you the systems, structure, processes, and skills to help you get the most out of your business and life.

THE IMPORTANCE OF MODELING

———

What is modeling and why is it so important?

Modeling is when you look at someone who is already successful in an area of life and you learn from the things they have done. This means you don't have to reinvent the wheel, and you can speed up your progress by learning from their mistakes and wins.

Take a step back for a minute...Just about everything we do is a learned behavior. We (consciously or not) watched how someone else did it and then tried it on our own. If you have kids, you've definitely seen this happen. I watched my boys do this their whole lives!

I bet there is at least one area in your life where it might be time to change that model. That's OK and changing your model is definitely possible. It starts with you being open to change, and the first step of change is through awareness.

Until you can admit that you need to change, it is really difficult to interrupt that pattern and create a new behavior. But after you realize you need to make a change, and know where you want to go, you need to find your model.

Who should you model?

When choosing who to model, consider how they excel in these areas: attitude, marketing, style, time, language, work, ethics, systems, teams, etc. Ultimately, you want to look for someone who has achieved a degree of success you'd like to achieve in a certain area (or areas) of life or business.

Next you need to visualize what your ideal business looks like...

What does your ideal business look like? How much money do you want to make? How much time do you want to spend working? How much stress (and what kind) are you OK with? That clear picture of your business helps you find the right model.

What's your timing/expectation?

I'm playing a new game with my kids called 1% per quarter. This means we set a goal where we improve by 1% each quarter. This is not a flashy, "quick results" kind of game. The focus is on long-term sustainable growth where change occurs over time. Choose the right time and expectation for the goals you want to achieve.

Use modeling.

One of my mentors Bill Mitchell told me, "It doesn't matter how you leave, it's how you arrive!" I want the journey of my life to be this insanely great experience of memories! I want you to chase after your goals and achieve the success you deserve.

COACHING AND MODELING—KEY AREAS OF YOUR LIFE

———

Have you ever played golf? I'm a big fan of hiring experts who you can model yourself after. I took a golf lesson recently and was feeling pretty good when I was warming up at the driving range. Most of the time I was getting some good distance, but every once and awhile the ball would hook or curve.

My coach gave me just a small adjustment in my grip and it completely changed the results! That's what a good coach does. They can identify problems and provide the right adjustments!

So what about your business? How big is the gap you need to adjust?

Here's the thing...You don't need a single silver bullet to radically change your business! The reality is that the change comes through making small adjustments that affect your business as a whole.

Quiz Your Business: Six Key Areas

On a scale of 1 to 10 how would you rank the following?

1. Database organization
2. Consistent contact of your database
3. Relevant, trackable marketing
4. Listing attraction marketing
   a. Database
   b. Geographic farm
   c. Open houses
   d. Expireds
5. Online marketing/conversions
6. Sales/influence skills
   a. Ability to set appointments
   b. Listing process
   c. Better consultation

What Got You Here Won't Get You There

If you remain where you are, you become irrelevant to the vast majority of buyers and sellers. The market and technology are always improving and you should be too.

Look at the previous list; where can you best improve? I don't want you to look for ways for this to be easier, but look for ways you can get better! Remember that the changes you make don't have to be huge. It is the small changes that often make the biggest difference!

NO MAGIC FORMULA FOR SUCCESS

———

People ask me all the time about the formula for success. They are hoping for some magic formula with lots of complicated steps. I don't think that exists, but I can tell you this...We are what we repeatedly do.

I've been coaching rockstar agents just like you for close to thirty years. There wasn't a magic formula that took me there, but I do want to show you what I did and what you can do too.

Three Steps for More Success in Your Life
1. Daily Training

Every day you need to train your body, soul, and mind!

Body: It is all about movement (exercise, yoga, running, etc.) and how you feel on the inside that radiates to people on the outside!

Soul: Do something that enriches you internally like prayer, meditation, etc.

Mind: Watch a great TED Talk or read a book! You have to fill up every day so you don't run on empty!

2. Quarterly Immersion Events

My goal is to always be growing and getting better. I know that when I get out of my own environment and attend an event, I learn even more. The alternative is focusing on the media, news, and negativity, and I don't want those things filling me up!

3. Private Coaching

I got my first coach when I was nineteen years old and I still have a coach today. If you want to reach the next level in your business and in your personal goals, coaching is one of the best things you can do. If you want to learn more about my coaching programs, visit TomFerry.com.

More of What You Want

I want you to have more of what you want in life. I'm going to say that again, because I don't think you caught it. I want you to have more of what you want in life.

For me that means being a great husband and a great father and I work on it every day. What does that mean for you? Are you willing to take action to get there? I know that greatness is already within you, and I'm asking you to step it up so that you can be the person you know you are capable of being!

{TOTAL CONVERSATIONS}

{# OF CONVERSATIONS}

{TOTAL CONVERSATIONS}

{9/10 MONTHS}

{# OF DAYS}

YOUR
DAILY #

CREATE CERTAINTY IN YOUR BUSINESS

—

KNOW YOUR DAILY NUMBER

What would it look like if you removed doubt, fear, and the unnecessary drama and anxiety from your business? What if you could have total certainty in your business? I have good news for you; it is possible!

It all comes down to knowing your daily number. Do you know your daily number? This is the daily number of calls you need to make to reach your ideal goal, and I'll show you how to calculate that number.

It all starts with your transaction goal... For example, let's say you want to sell thirty-six homes. Now comes the important part of marketing, tracking, and measuring.

This means you need to be data dependent, not dependent on your emotions.

To get to those thirty-six transactions, multiply it by fifty... That means you'll need to have roughly 1,800 total conversations to achieve your goal.

You'll then divide that number by ten months. I know what you're probably thinking, and yes there are twelve months in a year not ten! Let's be realistic, and take into account slow months, the holidays, vacations, etc.

You're already having conversations about the market in your day to day life. The shift comes through that "routine" that allows you to win and remove that doubt.

Next, divide by twenty-two days. Like the same calculation we did for months, we are taking into account days off, and only dividing by twenty-two.

This leaves you with a total of about **eight conversations per day.** Who should you call? Getting your calls is probably easier than you think...

Make four conversations to your database, and as you probably know, you should always be calling your database.

You can also make four calls to new leads. Think Zillow, leads you met at open houses, etc.

Finally, you should make four follow-up calls. Following up is one of the most important things you can do! I know it would be easy to keep reading on to the next section, but I want you to take action. Stop right now, and plug your numbers into this formula.

Is there uncertainty in the market? I think you can always count on a little bit of uncertainty, but there is a way to create certainty in your business. Calculate your daily number and get to work!

TOOLS FOR SUCCESS

If you were more organized, do you think you could double your income? Most people say yes, or know that more organization in their business will increase their profits. Here are some organization tips and tools you can start using today.

Digital Tools

Having digital tools can be a great way to stay organized. I know for some agents getting up to speed on the digital world can feel overwhelming. There are lots of tutorials out there, and simply looking at YouTube can help you find a lot of answers and ways to use the following programs, apps, and websites.

1. External Brain

Where do you house your ideas? Are they on a yellow notepad, buried on a laptop somewhere, or floating around in your head? Books like *Getting Things Done* and *Less Doing, More Living* are clear that you need to have a single capture device.

This is the one place where you store everything digital so that it is easy to search and find your information. I prefer Evernote but there are other tools too. Just make sure it is all in one place.

2. Project Management

Do you have a project management system you use in your office? I've talked to quite a few agents who use Trello.com. This is an easy digital system to manage your projects. It all resides in the cloud and is a great way to collaborate on a big project.

3. Scheduling Appointments—Digital Tools

Getting those clients on the phone and setting the appointment is hard enough, but you've got to schedule it too! There are a ton of digital tools out there that will help automate the process. Find one that is right for you and that makes the process easy for your clients.

Traditional Organizational Tools

Not all the tools I use for organization are digital. As you've seen in the #TomFerryShow, the walls of my office are whiteboards. This helps me brainstorm ideas, but whiteboards can be used for organizing too.

Check out these tools you can use on the whiteboard at your office.

Eisenhower Matrix

DO (NOW)	**DELEGATE**
PLAN (FUTURE)	**ELIMINATE**

The Eisenhower Matrix

The Eisenhower Matrix consists of four different boxes

to help you get things done. The boxes are Do, Delegate, Plan, and Eliminate. Here's how it works...

Do

In this box you write down three to five tasks. Keep it at this number because the more tasks you have, the less you will actually get done. Does that seem strange? Think about it this way...When you get two things done, you are almost halfway through your tasks!

Also, think about the items that you are going to be putting in this box. Is your business in revenue-generating mode or organization mode? Meaning, do you need to generate more revenue or focus on streamlining your business? Both are important, but where your business is at will help you determine your priorities.

Delegate

How much is your time worth? Seriously, stop and think about what your hourly rate is. Your time is valuable, and where you spend your time is really important. What tasks can you delegate? Can you pay someone $10 to $15 an hour to take care of the little tasks?

In this box you need to write down tasks that can be

delegated. Who you delegate these tasks to is up to you. It might make sense to hire to someone to work in your office. Or you could outsource to a virtual assistant or other service depending on the task.

Plan

In this box you are thinking about the long term. These are the things you need to take care of in the future. This is similar to the Do category, but includes projects that are down the line or more involved.

Eliminate

This category is tough for some agents. Take a step back and really think about the things you might need to eliminate. Start by analyzing your ROI. Are you getting two-to-one or five-to-one return on the money you are spending? Are you trying to do things simply because you heard someone else was doing them? Focus on what you are good at, and write down the things that you know should be eliminated from your business.

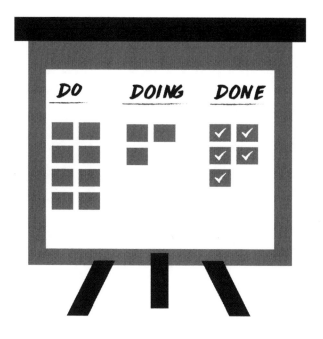

Do, Doing, Done Board

I've talked about my hero and mentor Mike Vance in the past. He was a legendary coach who worked with Walt Disney, Steve Jobs, and many others. He was the one who showed me the Do, Doing, Done board. For me, it serves as a great capture device for all of my ideas, and my team has this same board up at their desks.

How It Works

In the Do column, I usually have twenty-five to fifty ideas. Next is the Doing column, which has a maximum of three ideas that I am currently working on. The Done column is a great place to see the work you've completed!

Don't miss this last column...After you've completed a task, especially a big one, be sure to stop and celebrate. Take note of those wins and use them to fuel you forward toward your goals.

WHERE YOUR FOCUS IS

Wherever you put your focus, your energy follows. Stop reading right now and find some time in your schedule. This is time you are going to spend working on your business.

Did you catch that? Not working on *business*, but working on *your business*. This will help you know where you need to be more organized and focused.

Consider the following:

The Open Loops

Do you have any open projects going right now? I want you to close those "open loops" by first making a list and then prioritizing by what matters most. Not sure where to start? Go with the thing that you know will generate revenue. Once your list is prioritized, put time on your schedule to work on completing these projects.

From one entrepreneur to another, sometimes you have to just roll up your sleeves and get to work. It won't always be fun, but we both know that when those projects are finished, you'll feel more organized and be freed up to get more done.

Inbox "Zero"

Have you heard of that email strategy called inbox zero? It means that you have taken care of all your emails and don't have a ton of messages waiting in your inboxes. Start today by deleting irrelevant emails or moving your emails to folders so you can reference them later. The less cluttered your inbox is, the more efficient and effective you will be.

Declutter Your Social Newsfeed

Go through all your social media pages and unfriend/ unfollow those who are no longer relevant in your life. We all spend so much time on social media, and this time should be focused on the people who are relevant in our lives right now.

Schedule Your Next Quarter

You know your market, what type of marketing do you need to be doing to start the next quarter off right? Spend a few hours mapping out all your social posts, emails, social proof pieces, etc. This means that when that next quarter starts, you don't have to think, you just have to execute.

Updates on the Business
Active Listings

This is more than just looking at a list of your active listings. I want you to think about how to reverse engineer the sale. Think about if you had a similar listing in the past and the things you did that got it sold. Maybe even consider what you could have done differently last time that would have improved the process.

Pending Updates

Work with your transaction coordinator or take a look at where all of those pending deals currently are.

Your Service

Is there any way to improve your service? Like I'm always saying, what else can you do to provide more value to your customers?

Lead Gen Plan

Take a look at your pipeline. How many buyers and sellers are there, and do you have the right lead sources in place to keep feeding the funnel? You should also take a look at your marketing plan and see which areas need improvement and also take a look at those areas that are working. Be sure to read more about this in the Marketing section of the book.

People Updates

This is a great chance to get updates on your team, as well as the partners that help you get the win. You know that being in real estate is about relationships. What are the special, unique, or random acts of kindness you can do for those around you?

THE IMPORTANCE OF CHARM

———

Are you a "charming" agent? *Charming* means that you have an attractive or alluring quality or characteristic. Here's the reality...Anyone can be charming, and charming people do better with customers!

Five Steps to Charm

Here are five steps you can use to be more charming:

1. Build rapport.

Building rapport isn't only about connecting on common subjects; it is also about matching the feel of the person you are talking with. You should match their tone, volume, pace, posture, and language.

2. Be 100% focused.

Listening is a huge part of rapport building. It isn't just about listening with your ears; it is also about listening with your eyes and your body. That means that you are making eye contact, but not staring them down.

One of my first coaches told me to look at the person's right eye, look at their left eye, and then at their forehead or nose. You are still engaged without looking like you are a "stare-alina!"

Listening with your body is really about the posture you take. It means that you are leaning a little bit, showing that you are focused on what your customer is saying.

3. Engage through questions.

Listening taken one step further is about asking the right questions. You want to ask questions that help you get more context. So if you are taking a customer through a home, you want to ask them questions about the things they are excited about. Or if you are meeting someone new at a party, ask them context questions about how they were invited or who else they know at the party.

4. Be aware of spacing and touch.

You all know that person that gets inside your space! This person generates a little bit of anxiety and doesn't build rapport! You want to be aware of your spacing to ensure you aren't standing too close or too far away.

When you have started to build that rapport, a gentle touch to the arm or shoulder can build that rapport further. If you haven't built that closeness yet, beware, it could push your customers away.

5. Charismatic people are amazing storytellers.

You are probably already thinking of several people you know who are great storytellers and can win over a room with a great story. Stories are a great way to illustrate a point and connect with your customers.

CREATING YOUR UNSTOPPABLE SALES AND COMMUNICATIONS SKILLS

———

Your sales skills are incredibly important. It isn't just about closing the leads; it extends much further than that. Your marketing is only as good as your skills. If you have all the leads and don't know how to close them or what to say, you are paying too much for leads!

I want you to put a plan in place to develop your sales skills. Here are a few steps you can start taking today that will help you improve your sales skills.

The Training Plan for Building Strong Sales Skills
Pick one script to master at a time.

Scripts are great tools, and you should have your go-to scripts that you use in your business. It isn't enough to just have a list of scripts sitting on your hard drive or in a folder on your desk. You have to work on these scripts and know them.

Not sure which script to start with? Start with the most common objection or scenario that you hear most often and master that script first.

Spend ten to fifteen minutes a day reading the script out loud.

Communication is more than just the words coming out of your mouth. In fact, communication has three components: 7% is the words you say, 38% is your tonality, and 55% is your body language. If you want to learn more about that, check out Dr. Albert Mehrabian's study that he did while at UCLA.

Even though you can memorize a script, that is really a very small part of the message you are sending. That's why I recommend aligning your physiology with your words. You can even use your physical body to help change your tonality when you are on the phone!

For example, if you have a tendency to end your sentences with an upward tone, driving your hand downward in a chopping motion will help you bring the tone back down so you sound more confident. That downswing in tonality creates trust and authority.

Every day you need to practice that script. I recommend practicing in front of a mirror. Don't worry if you feel a little silly the first few times! Practicing in front of a mirror is something that great leaders and professional speakers have been doing for a very long time.

Take this one step further and video yourself. This doesn't have to be anything fancy, and you could even do it on your phone or laptop. If you are using a phone or camera, getting a tripod will make this process easier. The point of this exercise is to get better, but also see what your clients are seeing and hearing.

Find a few role-playing partners.

Practicing on your own is good, but practicing with others is even better. This will help you build up your confidence and better prepare when you meet with actual customers.

Remember that you aren't just role-playing the words...

Role-play the physiology (stance, posture, etc.) as well as your tone and pace.

I always recommend having more than one role-playing partner. This is because you will be able to practice interactions with different personalities and different objections.

Write out the script once a day.

This is an old-school memorization technique, but it is much easier to memorize a script when you write it out. Grab a pen and notebook and start copying that script over!

Having the script memorized is huge. When you have the script memorized, you can listen to the customer rather than thinking about what to say next. Our brains can only really focus on one thing at a time. Make sure that you are focused on your customer!

Record the audio of you reading the script.

Making an audio recording of the script in your own voice is a great tool for learning. You can do this on your phone and listen to it frequently. Listening to your own voice will help you memorize that script and even trigger passive learning.

Building Rapport

After you've got your scripts down, it is time to work on strengthening your rapport-building skills. You already know that people like to do business with people they know, like, and trust! I want to show you how to connect with customers in a way that removes the sales barrier in less than sixty seconds. If you want to be successful in real estate, you must master building rapport with your customers.

Listen to How They Answer

When you ask a question, be sure that you are really listening. For many agents, their default setting is to stop listening and start thinking about they are going to say next or even worse trying to get through their script.

I know that you are different, and I want you to step back and really listen. Remember, those same stats I mentioned about the words only being 7% of communication applies to your customers too.

Mirror or mimic.

As you're listening, you probably notice that everyone has a natural "style" of speaking. You want to try and do your best to match that same style.

Like I said before, if you are just thinking about what to say next you'll miss this...When you are relaxed and listening, this is felt by the customer. They can sense your confidence, and it shows that you are comfortable in your own skin. You are so comfortable that you can match their communication style and make them feel more comfortable.

Here are some things to consider when mirroring:

- Volume
- Words and patterns
- Tonality
- Rate of speech
- Emotional state

Validate your clients' answers.

It is incredibly important to validate your clients' answers. Think of this as basically repeating and approving what they are saying.

For example, you ask a client, "What is important to you in your future home?"

They answer, "We are looking for a place with three bedrooms, two baths, and a pool."

You say, "Excellent, so you are looking for a home with three bedrooms, two baths, and a pool."

When you repeat back that answer using the communication tips mentioned previously, you help take down that sales barrier! Everyone wants to feel validated, and this strategy helps the customer feel they are understood.

Know your customers' pain and know their problems.

Do you know your clients' pain points? These will vary based on the market and customer, but they are usually things like market conditions and past purchasing experiences. When you know their pain points, you can help create a solution that benefits them.

Practice, practice, practice.

If you want to be good on the phones, you have to practice. The last thing you want to do is practice on your customer. There is a confidence and a swagger you get when you know what to say when you are on the phones and in person. This also means that you will be more focused on helping your customers find a solution to their problems.

THE EXPERT'S GUIDE TO SETTING MORE APPOINTMENTS ON THE PHONE

———

Can I tell you a story? In my first three years of working in real estate coaching, I made a little over 158,000 calls working five and sometimes six days per week. I was making 150 or so outbound calls and talking to about thirty people every day. That first year I made $67,500, and I was excited! Before that I was working at a grocery store, and I had purple hair. My whole life had changed, and I had tripled my income!

It felt good to have such a massive income bump, but the second year I made almost the same amount of money.

Why? Because I did the exact same thing I did the previous year, and expected 3× the income! You and I both know that it doesn't work that way.

I knew that in order to get where I wanted to go I had to do things differently...I knew that I needed to get a coach, learn new methods, and put the right systems in place in order to achieve success with my appointment setting on the phone.

Fighting the Fear

Agents will often admit to me that they have a fear of the phone. I get it! Fear is a huge thing that no one wants to talk about when making calls.

Deep down most people fear being rejected. All those thoughts start going through your mind..."Oh no, what if they say no...what if they yes...?" Your anticipation of the response is getting in the way of your actions. You need to replace the "what if" questions with statements that keep you positive and focused: "If they say no, they're just not ready to sell/buy with me *yet*."

Also, next time you find yourself in a fearful state ask yourself the following three questions:

What's the worst-case scenario?

What's the most likely scenario?

What's the best-case scenario?

Your head is a scary place to be, and those questions will help you take back control. Fear has a way of letting small things spin out of control in our imagination, but we both know there is nothing to be afraid of on your next call.

The Three Best Ways to Create an Unstoppable Psychology for Prospecting

1. Always have more reasons to prospect than reasons not to!

Make a list of all the positive reasons you are prospecting. Things like removing the doubt and worry about your future income or even helping someone find their dream home.

2. Create massive accountability to take action; pain versus pleasure.

If you can find something painful that will motivate you, you are far more likely to succeed! I've had some of my coaching clients make a bet that if they didn't make their phone calls they would have to eat a can of cat food or donate to a political party they hated! The important part is that you have someone to hold you accountable.

3. Celebrate every time you do it!

It is all too easy to get caught up in the day-to-day work, but I want you to celebrate your wins! If you made it through your calls, get up and high-five your team!

Four Easy Steps to Getting More Appointments

Now that we've gotten the fear part covered, I want to give you the tools and tactics you can start using today to set more appointments and connect with your customers. It starts with these five easy steps:

1. Have an appointment-setting routine.

In order to get more appointments, you need to have a simple appointment-setting routine. It all starts with you knowing the answers to these three questions...

Why should this customer do business with me?

Remember all the value you are providing to the customer—how you help them get what they want (dream home, sell their current home, find a vacation home, etc.).

Think about it this way...The focus is all about helping the customer get the win, because when you do that you get the win too.

What am I committed to?

Getting clear on what you are committed to will help you frame why you are making the calls in the first place. I already know that you are committed to helping your clients, but you could phrase it into an affirmation. Something like, "I'm committed to helping twenty people achieve their dreams by purchasing a home this year."

That affirmation changes the tone of just making phone calls to helping families achieve their dreams.

What is my mindset for setting appointments?

Speaking of affirmations, are you saying them? Affirmations are powerful statements that will get you in the right mindset for success. I recommend that you start your day with affirmations, but at the very least say a few before you get on the phone.

One of my favorites is: "I'm a lean, mean appointment-setting machine!" Say it in front of a mirror and have it written down on a note card on your desk. Even better, make sure that you have a smile on your face when you say it!

2. Know your "automatic shot" and take that first.

When you look down that list of names in your CRM that you are going to call, a few of them should be automatic wins. These are calls that you know won't be too tough and will help you get the momentum to win the day.

So, if you absolutely had to get an appointment right now, who would you call first?

3. Be more assumptive with your language.

What you say absolutely matters, and your language should already assume you've got the win. You should say things like:

"When you list with me..."

"At our meeting..."

"When I sell your home..."

4. Get to the point!

Every agent I talk with has their own style, but the most successful ones all know this one key secret when calling prospects. They know that time is valuable and they get to the point quickly. For example: "I'm calling today to schedule an appointment..."

You probably already know this, but always give two options for setting a time. The client may offer up a different time altogether, but it makes things easy right from the start.

5. Close, because it's awkward if you don't!

Your customers are expecting the close at the end of the call. Here's the thing...You may have to close several times. In fact, some of the best salespeople have to close three, five, or seven times!

Most people have a natural barrier and are conditioned to reflexively say no on the phone. One of the best ways to defeat that is by simply saying, "Pencil me in at this time. Let me know if you need to change it later." It makes the whole process easy and friendly.

Create the Ultimate Appointment-Setting Environment

There is one more thing you need that will help you improve your appointment-setting ability...Your environment! I know it sounds silly, but here's the thing—your environment has a huge effect on your attitude and focus.

You want to create an environment that's focused on powerful actions. Here is how you can set your environment up for success:

1. Appointment Tracker—Visual

You want to track how many appointments you've made and what your goals are. Agents send me pictures all the time of the big boards they have in their office. This could be a big calendar, cork board, or even a whiteboard.

2. Appointment-Setting Shrine

Creating a small "shrine" is actually a lot of fun and a great reminder of why you are doing what you are doing. Use a foam presentation board, and it could even be one of the large ones that folds out into three sections. Think of this as sort of like a vision board with pictures of your family, how much money you want to make, and even a mirror.

3. Eliminating All Distractions

That messy desk isn't helping you set appointments! You want to remove all the distractions that will prevent you from making calls. This includes things like that blinking voicemail light, a big stack of papers, or having the Internet open with news, social media, etc.

4. Standing versus Sitting

Most of my team has stand-up desks, and I spend my whole day standing up. Why should you be standing? Besides the health benefits (I'm sure you've heard people saying that "sitting is the new cancer"), your body controls your tonality and your emotional state. Standing up can get you in the right state and even make your voice sound better on the phone. You sound more confident on the phone when you are standing up versus sitting down.

5. Music

Having a little music on in the background is a great way to help you get focused and keep your spirits up. I like Depeche Mode, but find or create the playlist that works best for you.

6. Plant

Having a plant in your office can help improve your mood. I have a few small succulents in my office, and I know agents who have larger indoor plants too.

7. Good Headset

This one seems like a no-brainer, but a good headset is an absolute must. I use a wireless Plantronics headset, but there are a ton of great headsets out there.

Don't Be Like Most Agents

Are you going to get out there and makes those calls or are you going to be like most agents...

Most agents haven't decided who to call.

You should have an active list of people you are looking forward to calling!

Most agents don't know what to say on the phone and fear rejection.

You know what to say and have practiced your scripts!

Most agents don't have a plan and have no idea how many calls to make or how often to make them.

You know your number and when to make to your calls!

Most agents don't have an environment set up for success.

You have all the tools you need to get on the phone and set those appointments.

Most agents don't align their personal psychology with the prospect.

You have the right self-talk, psychology, and attitude to win!

FEARLESS OBJECTION HANDLING

———

A few years back the failure rate for new real estate agents was 87%. The reason for this failure? Lack of sales training and fear!

The real root of the issue is that most people are afraid to handle sales objections and make the close, so they simply don't. When you know how to answer objections, they work to your advantage, because each objection will get you one step closer to the sale. Remember that objections mean customers want to do business with you; they just have questions they want answered.

Six Steps to Overcoming Objections

1. Get in the right state of mind.

Your face and your physiology affect your mental state. Be sure to check out the Mindset section of this book so that you are in the right mindset before making those calls or meeting with customers.

2. Start with an agreement.

The language you use with your customers is so important, and you have to start with an agreement. What does that mean? When your clients present an objection, you say things like, "I can appreciate that..." or, "I hear you..." After that, you want to create the connection, so you say things such as "You and I are on the same page..."

3. Transition.

After you've stated your agreement and made the connection, it is time for the transition. This is really simple but you have to understand the big difference between *and* versus *but*. The word *but* negates whatever comes before it. You always want to say something like, "I can appreciate that *and*..." Then you move on to the pattern.

4. Create a pattern.

The pattern is really taking the current situation and equating it to a familiar one in the past. Say things like, "Has there ever been a time when..." Have a customer think back to a time in their life that is similar to what you are asking them to do now and it didn't work out.

5. Come to agreement.

After you've followed those steps, you'll want to reinforce the agreement before you get ready for the close. Say things like, "Are we on the same page?" or, "Can we move forward?"

6. Close.

Now it's time to make "the ask" and go for the close! Remember, your clients are expecting this, and you have to close to get the sale!

Sample Pattern Script

When you put all those pieces together it looks something like this:

"I can appreciate that...and..."

"Has there ever been a time when (something similar happened) and it didn't work?"

"This time is exactly like that, can I explain (example)?"

"So, are we on the same page?"

"Then let's move forward and sign the offer."

CREATE YOUR MASTERMIND GROUP

Are you part of a mastermind group? If you are not familiar, mastermind groups are regular meetings of peers to discuss how you can improve your life and business.

This group will help you get motivation, brainstorm ideas, and even provide accountability. I've been a part of a mastermind group for years, and I recommend that you join one as soon as possible.

Why You Should Join a Mastermind Group

Mastermind groups aren't anything new. In fact, they have been used by Napoleon Hill, J.R.R. Tolkien, C.S. Lewis, and Jim Rohn. Jim Rohn actually said it best with this quote that I think about on a daily basis:

"You are the average of the five people you spend the most time with."

Don't miss that. Stop right now and think about the five people you are spending the most time with. Can you see them in your mind? You are the average of these five people.

Create Your Mastermind Group

If you want to really reach the next level, you might need to rethink the five people you are spending the most time with. That means getting specific and intentional about the group of people that will help you get more success in your business and your personal life.

So are you ready to create your mastermind group? Find five or six people who share your same level of determination, drive, and commitment, and start meeting with them regularly. Face-to-face is preferred, but you can also create a mastermind with people from different areas and meet online with Skype, Google Hangouts, or a similar program.

Not sure what to talk about in your mastermind group? Here are a few questions you can use to get the conversation started.

Mastermind Discussion Questions

- How do you survive when you're surrounded by deep discount brokers?
- How do you maintain relevancy when technology and rules change so quickly and so many competitors are entering the market?
- What are you doing to prepare for the market five to ten years from now?
- Do you see a trend of huge mega agent offices moving toward mom-and-pop offices?
- Which social media platform will dominate real estate in the next three to five years?
- What are the current trends in email marketing?

BUILDING YOUR TEAM OF ROCKSTARS

———

Everyone really wants to know what the future of real estate is! Let me tell you a little secret...The future of real estate is teams.

You and I both know that a team can outperform an individual. A team can also provide some freedom to your business because it means you aren't handling all the roles by yourself!

The Four Types of Teams

Let's start with the four basic types of teams:

1. The Illegitimate Team

I use this term somewhat jokingly. This team is really a collection of like-minded salespeople who have banded together to start selling. With this group there isn't a collection of different skill sets that really help a team thrive. The illegitimate team is more or less a group of salespeople with no one to run the operational aspects of the business.

2. The Family Team

This is the biggest segment of teams right now and is similar to what many people think of with the term *family business*. One of the biggest problems with the family team is that there are no set and defined roles. Also, when the family goes on vacation, the entire business goes on hold.

3. The Hero and the Minions

These are the rockstar agents who are incredible at what they do, but are also control freaks. They have high turnover on their teams and they burn out people quickly. It is the type of personality that wants to do everything, and doesn't usually play well with others.

4. The Team Builder

These are the agents who know their niche and they

do what they are best at, then hire experts for all other aspects of their business. They know that together they can grow and provide tons of value to their customers. This team structure is one of the best ways to maximize everyone's strengths.

The Two Types of Team Entrepreneurs

I've found that all team leaders see themselves as entrepreneurs, but they typically fall into two different categories.

The Artist: Artists are the vast majority of the people in the real estate business. They are high energy and creative, and their decisions are made from their gut and emotions. They are great on appointments and phenomenal with customers and negotiations. But when it comes to the organization of business, they are not as good.

The Operator: Operators are the people who work off of checklists, processes, systems, and numbers—less creative and more analytical. They are meticulous and detail oriented, and every file is arranged perfectly!

Neither of these personalities is good or bad, but a team needs both of them to be truly effective. I've found that the artists make all the money in this business when they have an operator. In order to have a successful team, you've got to have both. Are you an operator or an artist? Build your team accordingly.

Team Roles

Regardless of whether you are an operator or an artist, it is really important that you define the roles on your team. While each team is a little bit different, here are the most common roles in a team:

1. Buyers/Sales Agent

These team members work specifically with your buyers and sellers.

2. Transaction Coordinator

Your transaction coordinators are focused on the escrow side of your business.

3. Listing Coordinator

Your listing coordinator manages all the client and broker files and maintains weekly listing reports for the team.

4. Marketing Coordinator

Your marketing coordinator could be part-time or full-time, and this person is in charge of executing your marketing plan.

5. Operations Manger

Getting things done and managing projects are led by your operations manager.

6. Outbound and Inbound Sales Associates

You may have several sales associates on your team and they are in charge of making phone calls, setting appointments, and following up on and converting leads into appointments.

Your Hub

In addition to the individual roles on your team, there also has to be a hub. Think of the hub as the back end of a smart and successful real estate business.

The hub includes things like training, culture, branding, types of marketing, and even client satisfaction. The point is that when the roles and the plan are in place, you can totally scale and grow your team.

When to Build to Your Team

You know the power of a team, but the bigger question for most agents is knowing when to grow their team. Here are a few signs that will let you know if it is the right time to build or grow you team:

1. Your income has plateaued.

Leverage the assets of your business to make more money! People are always talking about the glass ceiling, because you only have so much time...Your time is one of the limits on how much money you can make. When your income has hit that plateau, building a team will help you earn more and better leverage your time.

2. You consistently miss your sales and listing goals.

When sales and listing goals are continually missed, many agents would simply think they are setting their goals too high. Instead, look at things differently, and find a way to produce more to reach those goals. A team is one of the ways you can leverage your assets to maximize your output.

3. You have no free time; you are running way too fast.

Do you ever feel like you aren't present for anyone? Like

you are being pulled in too many directions and time is going by way too fast? These are indicators that you need to slow down, and a team can help you do that.

4. There are cracks in your system/service.

Are your emails or mailers not going out? Or maybe you aren't following up with your deals. If the operation is breaking down or you aren't following up with your past clients and sphere, you need the help of a team!

5. All your eggs are in one basket.

When people get busy, they scale back on marketing and lead generation. This means agents put all their eggs in one basket. This is dangerous because trends could change, and it also limits growth.

6. You are averaging more than nine hours a day.

Are you working way too much? I'm not talking about putting out a few emergency fires, or working a long weekend. This is about consistently putting nine-plus hours into things you could outsource, like spending hours late into the evening hunting for leads; there is a better use of your time.

7. You are becoming tired and uninspired.

Could you carve out a few more dollars to buy some freedom? Will it get you to your goal faster or buy you some more time? Don't hit a point where you feel burned out and overworked.

8. You are missing out on your quality of life.

Are your health and vitality suffering because of your work? Are you missing out on the richness of life and those memorable experiences because you are overworked?

Your Team Outcome

So is it time to grow/build your team? It all starts with the outcome. What are you hoping to achieve? Maybe it means saving time or generating more money. You have to get clear on what you want to achieve.

With your goal in mind, you also need to set expectations by creating job descriptions. This means you'll know exactly what roles this person will fulfill and you can frame that when you interview them. Most importantly, you're going to be clear on what they are doing for you to free up your time so you can focus on the things that generate more revenue.

After you've done that, you've got to create a compensation plan. I recommend having a low base and a bonus based on closed transactions. Search online what an assistant makes in your area to get a good baseline for compensation.

The Babushka Doll

Have you ever seen Russian nesting dolls? Some people call them "babushka dolls." It is one big doll and then it splits in half and goes to a smaller doll. That smaller doll opens up to reveal a doll that is a little smaller and so on...

When most people hire someone, they look for someone to be the smaller babushka doll to their bigger one to make them feel important. It's a need for ego versus desire, and this trend continues when they add more people to their team.

We both know that if you want to do big things, you need to hang out with other people who do big things. So, the real key to leadership is to be that little babushka doll and find the big one and the next big one to grow your business.

TIME MANAGEMENT FOR SUCCESSFUL LEADERS

———

A few years ago I had a pretty amazing experience. I was in Mexico at a place called Bahia de Los Sueños owned by a friend of mine. After a wonderful evening and dinner, I came back to the resort and spent a few minutes with my boys on the beach. We were having a great time looking up at the stars and it led us to an interesting conversation about time.

My son asked me how old I was, and I said thirty-eight (this story took place a few years ago). Then he asked me how old I'd be when I died! Not something that you want to think about while you're on vacation! I told my son that the average life span is well into the eighties.

He reminded me that we don't have a lot of time. But the

bigger question is, "What are you going to do with your time?" This isn't just in the big picture over the course of your life...How are you going to spend your time on a daily or weekly basis?

Time is one of your most valuable assets, and how you spend that time is crucial. Are you spending your time on the things that matter or things that suck away your time? I want you to be taking action and moving toward your goals!

Without intentional action, you get stuck in what I've heard referred to as the "rocking chair" system. Meaning that you are moving a whole bunch but you aren't getting anywhere!

Use Time Wisely

When it comes to your time, think about the following...

1. What does your ideal week look like?

I've been talking about this concept for nearly thirty years, but you need to be living your life by design! This means filling your schedule with the important projects and people that will lead you to the kind of life that you want!

When you know what your priorities look like, you can start envisioning your ideal week. Think about how you are going to spend your time and start with the end goal in mind. You should also set an intention for your time, like "helping thirty-five families find a home this year."

2. Decide H.B.U.T. and delegate.

It is easy to just feel busy, but you have to direct your time to your priorities. I'm talking about what I like to refer to as "H.B.U.T." or the "highest and best use of your time." These are often the actions or activities that will make money like booking appointments, going on appointments, communicating (with your team, clients, partners, etc.), and managing your business.

The reality is that most agents spend 80% of their time on all the little annoying tasks. If isn't the highest and best use of your time, either don't do it or delegate it!

3. What adjustments do you need to make to your schedule to win?

Go back to your schedule...Maybe it is paper or digital, but take a look back at where you spent your time over the past month. You'll quickly be able to tell where your time is being spent.

Make sure you are spending more than 50% of your time on what matters most!

Turn Your Time into Money

Clear on your answers to those questions? As we've already talked about, time is one of your most valuable assets. On a very simple level, an asset is something that makes you money. I want you to be able to take your time and turn it into more money!

Let's dive a little deeper into some things you should stop doing and a few things you should start doing to get the most out of your schedule.

Drama

On the outer ring is all the drama of the day. Do you know anyone who gets caught up in drama? Maybe it is the person holding this book right now. As you already know, drama can be a huge distraction and prevent you from what really matters. You and I both know that whatever you focus on expands. So when you focus on that drama, it only gets bigger!

Organized

Organization is vital to your success, but it can also be a distraction. Yes, you need to have a marketing plan created, a CRM in place, and your schedule dialed in, but I know plenty of agents who fall into a different sort of organization trap.

Ever find yourself putting off an activity (like maybe calling a prospect) and instead, you start cleaning up your desk? You're cleaning up papers, putting folders away, and lining up your pens...Again, don't let this steal away your focus from the things that really matter. If you really need to get organized with the items mentioned in the previous paragraph, set some time aside and put it on your calendar to just focus on that.

Calls versus Contacts

So we've talked about how important it is to make those calls, but you have to have your focus in the right place... Making contacts isn't enough! When you focus on just making contacts, all you get is more contacts. The important part is getting more sales! You have to call your leads with the focus of turning those leads into sales.

Leads

You have to have leads. I've even seen some agents make these big lists with dollar amounts next to their leads. They create this big fantasy in their mind of how it is all going to be. This isn't a visualization strategy because no action is being taken! You have to call those leads. Then call them again! Then follow up with emails, mailers, and the other steps mentioned in your marketing plan.

Generating leads is important, and the reality is that there are a ton of ways to get leads, but what are you doing with those leads? Having a big collection of leads in your database or CRM isn't enough!

Appointments

What matters most? You've got to get those appointments, which turn into signed contracts. The only leading indicator of a healthy sales business is the amount of appointments you have in your schedule. Did you catch that? It is a cause-and-effect sort of thing! When your focus is setting appointments, guess what happens? You are on your way to getting more sales!

Making the Most of Your Time

I know what you're thinking..."Tom, I'm working on my

schedule, but I just need more time!" I get it; here are some tips to maximize your time.

1. Get up thirty minutes earlier.

I don't care if you already wake up at 7:00 a.m. Wake up at 6:30 a.m.! You know the old saying: "The early bird gets the worm." If you spend just thirty minutes a day improving yourself with a good book, meditation, and a little exercise, imagine the impact that would have over the course of a year!

2. Plan your day the night before.

Don't wait until the morning to figure out what your schedule for the day will be. Be prepared the night before so that your calendar in the morning is full of appointments and the right activities to be more productive every day.

3. Focus on dollar-producing activities.

There are four things we can do that are leading indicators of a healthy business, P-L-A-N. If you're following your plan to win, you're going to crush it!

- P—Prospecting (doing your hour of power, calling past clients)

- L—Lead follow-up (don't miss out on the chance to follow up on every lead and book more appointments)
- A—Appointments (you should be going on more)
- N—Negotiations and closing deals

4. Confirm appointments the day before.

Is there anything more annoying than a no-show? Whether it's over a text, phone call, or email, confirm every appointment the night before!

5. Know your outcome.

Before every meeting, project, or appointment, know what you want your outcome to be. What results do you want to produce? This technique will keep you focused every time!

6. Schedule more time off.

Every time you book a vacation, it seems like every buyer wants to buy and every seller wants to sell. If you give yourself a week, that's how long it will take to get things done. If you say, "I only have an hour then I'm gone for two days," there is a sense of urgency.

EARN MORE COMMISSION

———

Discount commissions are out there. A lot of agents are using this tactic to try to get more business, especially when the markets are good. Here's the thing: that is a lazy tactic. You and I both know that you are not a lazy agent, and you are doing so much work for your clients!

Your income is a direct correlation to the service you provide your customers. Here are some steps you can take to maximize your commissions and the value you are providing your customers:

Three Steps to Value

1. Do a competition analysis.

Take a look at the agents in your area and I'm sure you'll find lazy agents and discount companies. What are they doing? Look at their listing presentations, their marketing plans, and their websites. Analyze every bit of information you can.

You also want to look at their results. This includes things like list price versus sales price and maybe even transactions that fell out of escrow. There is a promise these companies and agents are making and you have to articulate the gap.

2. Identify the gap.

Identifying the gap means that you can clearly articulate to a client, "Here is what the other agents do, and here is what we do." This is often referred to as the law of contrast, and it allows you to show the value you are providing and the things you will do differently to help your customers get the win.

3. Build your case.

Show your customers why they should hire you! This

includes all of your unique selling proposition, the work you'll do every step of the way, and why you are a better choice. You also want to share with them what the discount companies are failing to tell them.

Take the 7% Challenge

I often refer to those steps as "taking the 7% challenge." Really though, this is a metaphor for earning the money you deserve for all of the great work you do for your clients. Every market is different, so if the norm is 4% commissions and you get 5%, then you are on the right track.

Ultimately I want you to step up your game, innovate, improve, create more value, and learn how to sell your services with authority.

HOW TO MANAGE YOUR FINANCES

———

Even though I want you to earn more commission and grow your business, managing money is something most agents struggle with. The fear of outliving your money is real, and no one wants to get to retirement and be flat broke!

Let's start by doing a forecast of the next ten years. Take this in the right light, and this exercise is really more about creating a financial plan. Think about your rate of increase and what you think you'll be earning over the next years and write it down.

Now, think about where that money should go. It should be divided up into three buckets:

1. **Tax Account:** Take one-third of every commission check and set it aside in a separate account just for taxes! That means that once tax season is here, you will have enough money in this account to pay your taxes without any other funds being disturbed.

2. **Your Personal Account:** Take another third of your commission check and put into your personal account. This account is just for paying your monthly dues, debts, vacations, and things you want to save for.

3. **Business Account:** Take the final third of your commission check and put it into your business account. This is for the day-to-day operations of your company but also to make sure your company is profitable in the future.

Bonus—Retirement: If you really want to set yourself up for a successful future, you've got to save for the future and invest in addition to these three buckets.

How Most Agents Manage Money

Working with agents for nearly thirty years, I've found that the average commission breakdown looks something like this:

Eighty Percent of Agents

The reality is that 80% of agents simply take their whole commission check and put it right into their personal account. This means that taxes, expenses, entertainment, and funds for the business will have to be sorted out later on. This is not a sustainable plan!

Fifteen Percent of Agents

About 15% of agents will do an equal spread between taxes, personal spending, and business costs. This is better, but it can make planning for the future really difficult.

Five Percent of Agents

Only 5% of agents follow this plan and think about the future. This means investing, and setting aside some money for assets like 529(b), real estate, stocks, bonds, retirement, etc.

YOUR STEPS TOWARD MASTERY

———

As you think about modeling in your career and your life, I want to share with you a concept that we will all spend our lives working on...mastery.

There is a huge difference between being interested versus being committed. Committed people persevere when things are difficult even when they don't feel like taking action.

What separates the wildly successful from the average? They keep going no matter what. They don't quit, and they continue to take action even when things are difficult.

Mastery is really built on your ability to persevere and continue getting better. It won't always be easy, and right now I want to encourage you to keep going. It will all be worth it, and I know that you can get the success you are striving for.

I'm sure you can think of something that you quit in the past. Maybe you even feel like quitting now. If you know the reasons why most people quit, you'll be better suited to handle the ups and downs when they arrive.

Why Most People Quit

1. Heart's Not in It

If your heart isn't in it, you won't last long. Oftentimes, we forget the reasons we started in the first place. Make sure that you've painted a clear picture of the "who" and "why" behind the goal you have set out to achieve.

2. No Support Structure

As an agent, I'm sure you've felt like you are alone at times. Real estate is by no means an easy career choice, but it can be incredibly rewarding. You have to have a support structure in place. This can be a team, an accountability partner, or simply someone you can call when that deal didn't turn out the way you thought it would. In life and business, we often think about what we want but forget to factor in the structure needed to achieve it.

3. The Tortoise versus the Hare

It is easy to look at someone else's success and only see the end result. You and I both know that success is a process and a collection of actions that are done over and over again. Like I always say, "Do the thing, have the power!"

You've heard that old story about the tortoise and the hare. When you can take consistent action, especially when no one is watching, you win.

I'm sure you're well aware that everything in life that is worthwhile takes time. Mastery is a process, and knowing the six phases of mastery will help you create a plan for success.

Six Phases of Mastery
1. Decide, Feedback, Plan, Tell the World

You've got to start with one really important question... What is it that you really want? Once you have your "why" figured out, you get feedback from your support system that we just talked about. After that, you simply create a plan and take action.

Sound easy? These steps aren't difficult to understand; taking action is the hard part.

Do you want to take your actions just a little bit further? I dare you to tell the "haters" in your life. You can bet they'll be there to remind you and ask you how things are going.

2. Ninety Days of Massive Action

Now that you know what it is that you really want, you'll start going after it. The first ninety days are super important. You've got to have the mindset that you will be taking massive action to achieve that goal. This time frame gives you time to collect data and figure out what works.

3. Momentum

Momentum can be an amazing thing that carries you forward, but there are a few things that will kill your momentum and massively slow down your progress.

The three biggest killers of your momentum are: your ego, having a breakdown, or a disaster. Ego can be kept in check by having the right mindset (be sure to check out the Mindset section of this book for more tips), but breakdown and disaster can't always be avoided.

You can't control everything in life, but you can control your reactions to breakdown and disaster. Know ahead of time that things might not go the way you planned on, but that doesn't mean it is over. Pick yourself up and get back to work. Setbacks are great opportunities for comebacks.

4. Stabilization

As you ride that momentum, you'll reach the stabilization stage. Things are leveling off, and it isn't a bad thing. This is your opportunity to put into practice the processes, systems, people, and communication to get to the next level.

Don't miss this...If you don't have these systems in place, you won't be able to handle the new levels of growth that are coming next. If you don't have the systems and processes in place, you'll end up swamped with work and not able to keep up with the growth.

5. The Quantum Leap

After things have stabilized, the next step is the quantum leap. All of a sudden, there is this huge explosion of growth! Like the stabilization stage before, you'll need to take another look at your systems to make sure they are ready for the next phase.

6. Mastery—Jedi Knight

At the very top is a level of growth that everyone wants

to achieve. When you hit mastery, growth occurs without you! I'm so incredibly proud of the growth achieved by my company, but I don't think we've reached the level of mastery yet. I'd say we are at stage 4 and getting better all the time.

Questions for You

Are you ready to take the steps to become a master? Take a few minutes and answer these questions. They will give you a good picture of where you are now and where you are going.

1. Which phase are you in?
2. Is your heart in it?
3. Do you have the structure and support to get to the level of success you desire?
4. Are you the tortoise or the hare?
5. Will you persevere through the process?

Mastery can be attained by anyone. It starts with you getting clear on what you really want, putting a plan in place to get there, and following through with the work to make it happen.

MARKETING

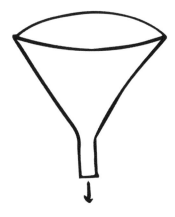

I've been blessed to learn from some amazing mentors like Mike Vance, who was the chief "idea and people development" executive for Walt Disney. Mike created out-of-the-box thinking that has shaped my mindset for life.

Like Peter Drucker, Mike believed "all business is innovation and marketing." It's so true! And I say, "The purpose of your marketing is to create appointments." So here is what I know, the number one predictor of success or failure is the number of appointments in your calendar right now.

Let me say that again, because I don't want you to miss it. The number one predictor of success or failure is the number of appointments in your calendar right now.

In my nearly thirty years of working with agents from all over the world, I've seen all sorts of marketing—the good, the bad, and the ugly. In this section, I've pulled together some of the best ideas, and I'll guide you through the proven strategies and techniques that have helped agents just like you become more successful.

YOUR UNIQUE SELLING PROPOSITION

You know as well as anyone that there are a lot of real estate agents out there competing for business! I see lots of agents just like you at my training events around the world, and they all want to know what they can do to stand out among the competition.

It starts with knowing your USP! What's your USP? That stands for *unique selling proposition*, and it is what makes you and your business unique. Do you know your USP right off the top of your head?

Know Your USPs

Here's the thing...If you don't know your USP, it can have serious impact on your business. Here are some of the things I've seen from agents who don't have a good grasp on the unique ways they can help their clients.

Insecure: If you don't know what makes you and your business unique, you will be insecure. When you are insecure, you are in your head. This means you are thinking about you! You aren't sure what to say and do next. Instead, you should be focused on the value you can provide your customers and how you can solve their problems.

Hoping: You've been there before...Every presentation you go on, you are hoping to get lucky and that they will say yes. Hope is not a good strategy.

Just Another Realtor: There are millions of people with an active real estate license. If you go into the MLS, you will see a ton of realtors who have never sold a house. The main reason for this is because they don't stand out among the sea of people in the marketplace. You don't have to be like them.

When You Know Your USPs

When you know your USP, everything changes! Here's how it will impact you and your business...

Confidence: People are naturally attracted to those who

have confidence, and let's be honest, confidence is sexy! When you can state with authority why someone should work with you versus the competition, it makes a huge difference! Your confidence comes through and makes it almost impossible for the other person to deny it. But be warned, too much confidence is the opposite of sexy.

Certainty: At the end of the day, when you're presenting to a potential client and you know the difference between you and your competition, you will have certainty. Your potential clients are looking to make money or save money (buyer or seller) or time (save them time or sell their home faster), and they need to know with certainty that you are the one to help them do one or the other or both.

Better Experience: Ultimately, when you know how you can help your customers, they'll choose you over the competition. When you deliver on those USPs, you are providing a better experience for your customer. That means more referrals and more sales in the future.

GETTING NOTICED IN A CROWDED MARKETPLACE

Even though there are a ton of real estate agents competing for business, the 80/20 philosophy still applies. Have you heard of this before? This basically means that 80% of the sales are handled by the top 20% of agents.

I'm sure you've even talked to a lead and they say something like, "Oh, I've got a friend in real estate…" If they didn't know someone in real estate, you might think they didn't have any friends! I'm joking, but you know how important it is to distinguish yourself when so many agents are looking for business.

In addition to knowing your USPs, there are a few other things you can do to separate yourself from the competition.

Three Steps to Attract Customers

1. Get to know your customers.

It is an old saying, but people really want to work with someone that they know. This starts with you first really understanding and getting to know who your potential customers are. Who are the people that want to sell their homes in your area? What is important to them? How do they want to be communicated with?

This goes for people who want to buy in your area too. What age group do they typically fall in? What is important to them in buying a house? How do they like to be communicated with?

2. Your customers have to like you.

You need to get to know your customers, and after you've gotten to know them, they can start to like you. Don't overthink this!

Start by finding some sort of common ground. Think sports, local places (restaurants, points of interest, etc.), family, a local charity, or hundreds of other things. If you've done your research on the first step, this shouldn't be too hard.

3. Your customers have to trust you.

We both know that if you want to get that listing, the customer has to trust you. Trust can be a tough thing to earn, and there are a few simple things you can do to create that trust faster.

Make sure you have some social proof like "just listed/ just sold" pieces, Zillow reviews, testimonials, or simply demonstrating your local knowledge of the area. You should even have an "About" page on your website with more information about you and a video.

If you want to leverage these methods even more, use Google retargeting ads so that you are creating that familiarity with your image and brand that follows your customers around the Internet. If you have been to my site before, you've probably seen my ads on the sites you are visiting afterward!

The Next Steps

After you made it through those first few steps you can start making some progress with your leads. But know this...Even after you've built that trust, it isn't over yet. You've simply won the option for your customer to try you out.

Don't forget to see this from your customers' perspective. They are trusting you to help them with one of the largest financial decisions they will ever make. When they like you, trust you, and know that you are committed to helping them, it makes everything so much easier. If you served them and did a good job helping them find a solution, you'll get repeat business and referrals in the future.

THE HONEST TRUTH ABOUT MARKETING

Have you noticed that marketing is changing? Yes, providing value in an engaging way is still what rules the day, but how you send the messages is different. The mediums will always be changing and evolving, but here are a few things you should know about marketing right now.

Marketing Today

1. It's a new game.

The old game is stimulus-response. I send you a mailer, and then expect a phone call. You've seen this a hundred times...All of the real estate marketing agent pieces that say, "CALL ME!!!!!!" That stuff kind of worked in 1990 but not today. The stimulus is still there, but the response is of course what we are after.

Today the consumer has too many choices, too much stimulus. This means that once you get leads to click through to your website, you have to provide them what they are looking for or they are gone! Customers want to see how many reviews you have, view a track record of success, and make sure that you are the right agent to help them.

Ultimately this is about credibility and having the customer respond to the stimulus the way you want.

2. Have a multichannel approach.

You have to have a multichannel approach, whether it's a phone call, a Facebook private message, or even a display ad. Each one of those is only producing a certain result, and if you put all your eggs in one basket, all you're doing is limiting your own income.

The multichannel approach will help you leverage your reach across different social platforms. You can still share the same sort of content, ideas, and marketing, but you'll now be exposed to a much larger audience.

3. Stop romanticizing.

You can't romanticize about the work that has to be done. I talk to agents all the time who say, "But, Tom, I don't like doing direct mail!" or, "But, Tom, I'm not good with the computer; this is the way I've always done it."

No one cares that those agents don't like it. The question is, what does the customer want? And most importantly, what is producing the best result?

4. Always be testing.

There's no failure, only a result. So if you send out 1,000 emails and no one responds, it's not a failure. It just means the subject line didn't work. Or maybe there wasn't anything in the copy of that marketing message that triggered a response.

Don't miss this...If that email didn't get the desired result, don't look at it as a failure. This is your opportunity to ask some questions. What are three different headlines you can test? What are three different calls to action that you can test? That same methodology applies to video, to Facebook ads, to email marketing, to making phone calls, and to trying different dialogues.

The bottom line is this: ABT or *always be testing*. So what does that mean? If you send an email to your entire database of 1,000 people, 500 people will get one subject line and 500 will get a different subject line. Then you look at the results and see which subject line produced the best results.

REACH YOUR AUDIENCE THROUGH DIGITAL MARKETING

———

How is your digital marketing going? Whether you are sharing a new listing or simply looking for leads, your social media and digital marketing has to be dialed in!

Check out this plan that I have assembled; you can use it to reach your audience on their favorite social sites, share your listings, and provide value to your customers. The idea is to create a multichannel approach to sharing your content.

Digital Marketing Plan

1. Authenticity

You have to be authentic! Remember that you are interacting with real people. Make sure that you know your audience and remember that it is important to be yourself. You don't have to puff yourself up or pretend to be someone else. Focus on providing a solution to your audience.

2. Consistency

Consistency is everything! That means sending out content at regular intervals, because your fans are expecting it. If you post a link to your blog on Thursday or a video every weekend, keep doing it! This is the way you build trust and grow your audience.

3. Response and Engagement

Show that you're listening and appreciate all engagements. Be sure that you are responding within twenty-four hours. Even if it is just liking their comments, it lets your clients know they are appreciated.

4. Quality and Good Marketing

Everything you do is representative of your brand. It's your brand! How do you want to represent yourself and your business? Your marketing is part of your legacy and should be an accurate depiction of your integrity, your passion, and your ability to sell a home!

The content you make should look great! Not skilled at graphics or writing good copy? You can hire a freelance person (or virtual assistant) to create content, or maybe consider hiring someone part time to help.

The Best Free Tools

If you have a marketing team, they are probably already using these tools. But if you are handling your own social media posting and management now, I think you could really benefit from using the following tools.

1. Sprout Social, Hootsuite, or Buffer for Scheduling

At the time of this writing, scheduling tools like Sprout Social, Hootsuite, or Buffer are great for advanced planning. This will allow you to stay consistent on your publishing schedule and post while you are out doing other things.

However, it's important to stay relevant and review your scheduled posts often. As you get to know your audience, you can schedule posts for the times when they are most active on social media.

2. Bitly for URL Tracking and Shortening

There are several different link-shortening websites out there, but my team and I use Bitly. This allows us to shorten links and track where they came from. It also lets you know how many clicks each link got, which days received the most clicks, and the social platform the clicks came from.

You can create an account for bit.ly links, and you can also see the effectiveness of each link by typing a "+" after the URL to see the stats.

3. MailChimp for Email Marketing

Which email platform you use isn't really important, but the important part is that you are sending emails out to your database. MailChimp is one of the simplest email marketing programs for small businesses, and it is pretty easy to use.

4. Google Analytics

Google Analytics gives you data into where your Web visitors are coming from, how long they are staying, which pages have the most traffic, and much, much more! They also offer a simple online certification to help you master setting up your account and analyzing the data.

Use the data to get a better picture of how people are using your website and as a way to continue providing them with content they find valuable.

Taking Action

The tools you use and the platforms aren't what matters... This is just another way for you to provide value to your customers and engage with them on the places they are spending time online.

STORYTELLING FOR MARKETERS

———

Think about a really great story. Maybe it is a great movie, book, or story that someone told you. The thing about great stories is that they have the ability to change the way we think and feel, and they provide an emotional connection to the storyteller. **Are you harnessing the power of your story to better connect with your clients?**

I was talking to my good friend and coauthor of my last book, *Life! By Design*, Laura Morton. She is a storytelling expert and has written fifty-four books; twenty of them are *New York Times* best sellers.

Laura says every great story must have these important elements:

- Every great story must be irresistible, memorable, and believable.
- Every great story must have conflict and resolution.

So how can you use stories in real estate? It could be as simple as a review, case study, or retelling of any time you saved the day and solved the problem.

How to Tell Your Story

Telling your story doesn't have to be difficult. Laura recommends you stick to these three strategies to best tell your story.

1. Know *your message* before you start and work backward from there.

Like any great story, you have to have a hero! It could be you or the customer or someone else entirely. You want this story to relate to your audience or the situation at hand. You don't want to come up with the stories on the spot if you don't have to, so have a few examples of stories that would be applicable.

Maybe it was a similar situation where you helped another customer find their dream home or helped solve some problem along the way. You might want to take a few minutes to think about past stories where you got the win for your customers.

2. Write and talk about what you know.

Stories need to be authentic and truthful. These stories should be rooted in your experience, and the more details you can provide, the better.

Know that the more believable your story is, the more you will connect with your audience.

3. Show more, tell less.

Now that your story has a hero, is relatable to the situation, and is believable, it is only missing one very important element! You have to have a memorable element and resolve the conflict in the story. This is where you get to show off how it all worked out and how you rode in on the white horse!

Telling Stories

I'm sure you've noticed that I tell stories all the time. They are a great way to illustrate a point and build rapport. I know you have a great story, and it can be the thing that helps separate you from the competition.

GROWTH STRATEGIES

———

You want to know a secret? "The local market knowledge is the most important consideration of a buyer when selecting an agent." I found this in a recent Zillow Consumer Report, and most agents don't even realize that fact! Even more interesting is that the vast majority of customers found their agents and their home online!

Advertising for Your Business

Nowadays, the ad spend it will take to get your potential customers to click on an ad is bananas! We are all arbitraging ads, but I want to talk to you about your customer database. Don't make your strategy strictly referrals, and think about these important questions for your business:

- How can you stay top of mind in the most relevant way with your database?

- How can you intelligently share your expertise and experience?
- How can you generate more referrals and direct transactions?

How do you find the answers to those questions? Start by making an avatar of your database. Who are your customers, and what problems are they facing? Create the stats and paint a picture of who they are.

Put yourself in their shoes and think about how they would answer these questions:

- What are your thoughts on the future of housing?
- Do you plan on living in a bigger house or a smaller house and why?
- What is important to you in a home today, versus when you bought yours?

Once you've dialed in who your audience is, here is how you can better connect with them through that multi-channel approach.

This is how that looks across a few of the biggest channels:

Phone Calls

Agents love making phone calls, but even if you're calling your database, two out of ten answer the phone. That's the game today. Most people are busy, and simply inclined to respond in a different way. It doesn't mean you shouldn't call your database; just expect about 20% to answer the phone.

At the very least, make it a point to call your entire database every quarter. Because if you don't contact them at least once a quarter, you'll lose that relationship.

Email

If you're an email ninja, you're getting a 17% open rate. But that doesn't mean 17% of people actually respond to your emails; they just opened it up. A realistic response rate? Maybe 2% to 5%. If you're talking about thousands of people, this is still a worthwhile return.

Text Message

I've spoken with many agents who are part of my coaching program, and they have found that text messages had a great response rate. I surveyed thousands of agents, and the reports showed that text messages had a 95% response rate in under five minutes. This will likely change in the future, but for now, a 95% response is amazing!

Direct Mail

Direct mail is old school, and yes, I'm actually talking about putting stuff in the mail! That same survey showed a 3% to 5% response rate to direct mail. That is phenomenal today!

Want to hear about a mailer that works? Go to Zillow and type in your lead's address. Print out the Zestimate page and highlight the amount. Then write out a handwritten note that looks something like this:

"Dear (name), I know your home is worth more than (Zestimate amount). Want to know your home's real value as of today? Call, text or email me."

You can mail it or slide it under their door. My coaching clients have told me that they are getting one out of five people calling them because everybody wants to challenge the value of their home.

Video

Video is playing a stronger role in the social space, and

it's a great way to get the word out. I'm sure you're not thinking this, but maybe you know someone who would say, "But, Tom, what if I do a video, and no one watches?" Here is what I would say to that "friend" of yours..."Who cares how many people watch it? You just want the right person to see your message."

As a quick side note, Facebook is a great way for you to demonstrate your local market knowledge and reach your audience. Do a quick monthly update with the important, relevant information to your database.

Facebook Look-Alike Audiences

So, think about this...You've got your 345 friends on Facebook, and you're running ads to them. They're responding to you and sending private messages. You're bringing them value and talking about what they want to know most, which is the value of their home.

Now consider this, Facebook allows you to create a look-alike audience. That means that you take your 345 people and Facebook can pair you with, let's say, 10,000 people that look and behave just like the people inside your database.

People want to work with people who are just like them.

The assumption is that the look-alike audience will give you people that are into the same types of things.

Database Integrity

Do you have database integrity? In your phone, you have a Bob at 310-555-1212, but you don't know his last name. Maybe you don't know where he lives, or really anything else about him except his phone number. There are services out there like Intelius.com or Fetch through GeographicFarm.com that will help you fill in the gaps. They use the information pieces you already have, and now you know Bob is Robert Jones and lives at 123 Humma Humma Street in Irvine. You've got all his data, and now you've added some more integrity to your database.

There's No Wrong Way

There are multiple channels and ways to reach out and connect with people. There's no wrong way to do it. The mistake that most agents make is not casting a large enough net. My point to you: look at all these different ways that you can reach out and engage with people. I know that we all want more referrals, but remember that you have to take care of your database so that your referrals consume data first.

THE MEGA OPEN HOUSE STRATEGY

—

You and I both know there are really two ways to hold an open house. You can hope and pray to the real estate gods and run a few ads in print or digital media...and no one shows up.

Or you can hold an open house the Tom Ferry way and throw a mega house! This means you invite all the neighbors, invite your database, and invite tons of others with the promise of food and a good time!

Mega open houses are actually a lot of fun, and I've talked to agents who have hired food trucks, had the event catered, brought in bounce houses and other kinds of entertainment.

The benefit to you is that you are getting people who are potentially interested in purchasing the home like a regular open house. You are also getting the ability to grow your database by connecting with the neighborhood and giving them a reason to attend an open house event.

Invitations to the Open House

Here's everything you need to know to get people at your next mega open house:

1. Create a short-form (sixty seconds) video and email the video as an invitation to your database.

Send this at least forty-eight hours before your open house.

2. Create a Facebook boost or ad about the open house.

The boost/ad gives you the ability to target your audience based on geography, income, if they have children, age, and more!

3. A day or two before the open house, go door-knocking to invite neighbors.

Have a flyer to hand the neighbors that has a photo of the house and the price. Introduce yourself, explaining that you just listed the neighbor's house and you wanted to give all the neighbors the opportunity to see the house before anyone else.

Maximize Buyer and Seller Leads at Your Open House

Once all those leads show up at your mega open house, you need to have a few questions ready to ask them!

1. "How long have you been searching?"

Straightforward and easy, this will help you get the conversation going, and you can follow up with more questions.

2. "What does your ideal home look like?"

The leads will now start to open up and tell you more about what they are looking for. They are essentially telling you their problem, and it is up to you to provide that value and help them find a solution.

3. "I see a lot of homes before they hit the market; are you interested?"

This is a great way to show that you can help your customers and have some additional value to offer.

Interacting with the Neighbors

In addition to the new leads coming over, neighbors will be coming to the mega open house, too. Many of them will likely want to know what their house is worth compared to your listing. The goal is to add these people to your database.

You can add neighbors to your database by having a few iPads set up at your mega open house with a big sign that says, "Want to know the value of your home?" They can sign up on the iPad and that sets you up with a reason to reach out in the future.

Besides the database, building rapport with the neighbors is really important. Here are a few questions you can ask that work really well:

"How long have you lived here?"

"Where are you from?"

"How did you pick this area?"

"If you were to move, where to next?"

After that, find out what the client's needs are.

"Most of our clients want to know their home's real value because (refinance, move, rental, relocate, just want to know...); how about you?"

Your Next Open House

It is that easy! Just make the whole event fun and provide some value. Do me a favor, when you try this out, be sure to send me a tweet @TomFerry and let me know how it goes!

EXPIREDS

What if I told you that I finally found the needle in the haystack? I want to show you how to find those needles that are in the haystack of your marketplace.

The needle is actually something that many agents are afraid of! Don't worry, it isn't scary, and I'm going to give you the formula to conquer it.

So what's the needle? Expireds. Some of you are already thinking about closing the book, but I don't want you to miss out on a lead source that many agents don't even know how use!

Why are agents so afraid of expired listings? It really comes down to two reasons.

The first is the fixed mindset where your mind goes crazy

and tells a story about expireds. You start to envision all the awful things that could happen and that leads to the second reason...

From here, fear takes over and prevents you from taking action! Maybe it is because you don't know what to say, or you worry about taking the rejection personally. Don't take on that transference of emotion, and add this great lead source to your playbook!

Connecting with Expireds

So, if you're willing to adopt that growth mindset and push those fears aside, you'll see the true heart of the matter. Remember, these are potential clients who need to be served just like anyone else.

When you call an expired, you are calling someone who has an unmet expectation and who now has a rise in an emotion because of the whole scenario. You can't take this personally, and know that when these customers are upset, it isn't about you.

Put yourself in their shoes, and use some of these tips...

How Do You Win?

Start by making a choice. You can't work all of the expired listings, so just cherry-pick the ones you want. This means you see the needle in the haystack and see the areas where you can bring value.

Moving forward, you simply need to ask the right questions. Customize them based on your audience/area, but here are a few examples:

"If I brought you an offer yesterday to sell your home with terms that are desirable, where are you moving to?"

"If I sold your home in the next thirty days, would you still like to move?"

"So, if I could, would you be willing to meet with me for twenty minutes to show you how we sold thirty-one homes? Ten were previously listed with other agents and sold for 99% of list price in an average of twenty-three days, and every one of those sellers gave me a five-star review. Would it be worth twenty minutes of your time?"

"What's important to you in the next agent you choose?"

If you are really serious about finding those needles in

the haystack and taking action, you need to create a killer marketing piece just for expireds.

Your marketing piece should have the following elements:

- Picture of the house with all the details (address, previous number of listing agents, days on market, etc.)
- Listing by your team (after expiring)
- Executed marketing plan
- Thousands of online views
- A large number of agents at preview
- Close to two hundred buyers at open house
- Three offers
- Sold at 99% of list price
- Sold in less than a month
- Five-star review

The Needle

So where do you find the needle? That needle in the haystack you've been looking for is right in front of you in the MLS!

Take the time and look back at the expired listings. Remember that you don't have to work with all of them, just cherry-pick the ones you want. Do you have it in your head and do you have it in your heart to serve those clients?

HOLIDAY MARKETING STRATEGIES

———

Do you have a holiday marketing plan in place? This could really be for any of the major December holidays or holidays throughout the year. This holiday marketing plan is different than the one you wrote at the beginning of the year.

Ask yourself, "Knowing what I know now, what are the most impactful marketing activities I can do in this short window of time?"

Think about what kind of adjustments you need to make to your marketing to make it more relevant for the holidays. Here are a few examples you can use for the December holidays:

- Thinking of selling next year?
- Schedule an appointment for January.
- List eight reasons to sell during the holidays.
- "Thank you! We helped (x) families buy and sell last year."
- Create a map with all the properties you've sold!

Also get specific with what you are going to do...Meaning you know how many emails, mailers, open houses, and calls you will be doing.

Like I always say, make sure this special holiday marketing plan is up and visual in your office.

Bonus tip: My friends over at 3 Day Blinds have done extensive testing around marketing during the winter holidays. Do you know what got the best response with their customers? Snowflakes! Make sure you add them to everything in your December marketing!

Creating Your Holiday Marketing Plan

Here are a few things to think about when creating your holiday marketing plan:

Are you sending a gift?

Make the gift (and delivery) meaningful and special. Not sure who you should send gifts to? Consider sending a gift to:

- Clients under contract
- Best referral sources
- Partners
- Your top clients from this year or last year

Are you doing an event?

I'm a big fan of holiday parties! I talk to agents all the time who throw big mega open houses during the holidays, Easter egg hunts, or even Halloween parties. I've heard of one agent who lived in a warm climate who trucked in snow and Santa and the whole thing for an amazing experience.

Things to Think about for Your Holiday Party

- Theme
- Who's involved
- Prizes and surprises
- Location

Give Back

This is a great time to make a donation to your community, church, or favorite charity. Remember that the donation doesn't have to be a check...There are all sorts of unique ways you can give back through your time, donating of goods, or sponsoring an event or program.

HOW TO ATTRACT
MORE LISTINGS

———

Are you aware of the power that comes from your words? You've probably heard it said before, but what you say matters. In fact, the questions you ask directly affect how many listings you are able to get. I want to share with you three questions that will impact your ability to take more listings.

It doesn't matter if you're at the coffee shop, a cocktail party, or simply calling an expired listing—these are the questions that you'll want to ask everyone you are having a conversation with!

Three Questions for More Listings

Question #1: Have you had any thoughts of selling?

It seems like a simple question, but it is direct and straight-forward, and it works. Remember to ask and then just sit back and listen. Because here's the thing—everyone has thought about selling, but it all comes down to timing. As a bonus to this question, try asking, "Are you currently living in your dream home?"

Question #2: Do you know anyone who's thinking about selling?

There's referral opportunities everywhere! This question could open lots of doors to potentials sales. Be sure to add a few thought joggers to help people frame their response. Say something like, "This could be people you work with, know from church, family members, friends, or even your neighbors."

Question #3: At what price would you become a seller?

Regardless of market conditions, nearly everyone has that "number" in mind. This is a great conversation to ask any homeowner. The key is to inquire and serve your clients accordingly.

Take Action.

I know it is easy to read these questions and then keep moving on in the book, but that isn't enough...You've got to take action. Write out these three questions on an index card or sticky note and have them up in your office. You can put them in your wallet, and even put them up on your bathroom mirror. These are the questions you should be asking everyone!

Additionally, you should add them to the list of things you role-play with other agents. Make sure you've got these practiced and ready to go. Be confident when you ask, and remember the most important part is to always be providing value for your clients.

THE SECRET TO ATTRACTING MORE LEADS

There is a serious problem that almost every agent faces when it comes to leads. You are losing more money than you are earning! So the question is, how much money are you leaving on the table?

Of the thousands of agents we have surveyed, our numbers show that the majority of money and conversions are made in the follow-up! Only 5.6% of leads are converted on the first contact, and 68% of leads are converted after eight to twelve conversations!

Think about it this way...You might have a small amount of leads at the moment, but it seems like shortly thereafter you are flooded with a bunch of leads! So you get all those leads, and find the one or two that you like. If you are like most of the agents I talk to, you focus on those easy leads, but you are missing out on a ton of upside potential!

Three Ways to Win More Leads

Here are three things you can do that will keep you from leaving money on the table:

1. Have a long-term follow-up campaign.

Think about a funnel of those eight to twelve conversations you could be having with the leads. It doesn't even have to be phone calls, it could be emails, BombBomb videos, or text messages. The point is that you have to have a strategy in place for the long term. Because we both know, if you want to be an anomaly in this business, you have to act like one!

2. Be aware.

Remember 68% of leads are converted after eight to twelve conversations. Most salespeople don't realize how many conversations are required to close a lead, and they quit early on. I want you to be aware of this fact, so that you can put a plan in place to hit those eight to twelve conversations.

3. Don't settle for "layups" when "blowouts" are possible.

Don't settle for something small! Let me say it again, because I don't want you to miss it...Don't settle for something small. Yes, it is easy to follow up with a few of your favorite leads, but I don't want you to leave that money on the table. Make the calls, have the conversations, and be the agent that follows up to get the win!

The big win is totally available to you, but you have to have the mindset to go after it! As I always say, "Do the thing, have the power." Go after those leads and go for the blowout!

IMPROVE YOUR LISTING PRESENTATION

———

How's your listing presentation? When your listing presentation is solid, your confidence improves, too. I'm about to share with you five ways to dramatically improve your listing presentations. But you need to know something first...

Remember that quote from *Spider-Man*, "With great power, comes great responsibility." These are some powerful sales techniques, and I know you can use them to greatly impact your conversion and sales rates.

These methods can work in your favor, but you've got to do the work ahead of time. This means putting in some time to do the research, practice your skills, and look for ways to add that value to your customers.

Prequalify Your Customers

It all begins with getting to know your customer before the appointment. Do a little research about them on social media sites (no, this isn't considered stalking), so that you know what their personality is like as well as some things they might be interested in. You want to find those commonalities so that you can build rapport easily.

You also want to prequalify your customers. This doesn't have to be too complicated and should cover some of the following topics...

- Who are the decision makers?
- What are their exact needs and desires?
- When are they looking to make a decision?
- What is your plan B if it doesn't work out?

Do Your Homework on the Market

It isn't enough to just know the customer, you also need to know the market, too. This means going beyond the comps. You should know the features of the property, the neighborhood, the culture, the community, and everything else!

Show Up Mentally Prepared

You know how important your psychology is, and like I always say, "Your head is a scary place to be!" You have to be mentally prepared when you show up to meet with you clients.

Know this...If you show up late, you'll be out of rapport with your clients instantly. You have to be on time, and I recommend leaving at least fifteen minutes earlier than you think you need to.

You can get in the right head space by visualizing your desired outcome of the meeting with your customers. If you need some visualization tips, be sure to check out the Mindset section of this book!

You don't want to be overconfident in this meeting, but you want to have the assumption that you are going to get the "Yes" from the customer.

Tell the Story

Stories are incredibly powerful and can be a way to prime the customer to be engaged with the value you are providing to them. It will give you permission to help move the customer to a mutually desired end result.

Your story can be one of the things that makes you stand out from the competition out there. Create a story that sounds something like this...

- "I've been on sixty-two of these appointments and fifty-eight people chose to work with me. My goal is to make this process as easy and quick as possible for you."
- Or if you're a newer agent: "Our firm has successfully listed and sold over 275 homes, and every week at our team meeting, we debrief. We discovered there are five questions that every customer asks. Would you like to know what they are?"

Remember to create the story around your customer. Think about how they would see it and really view the story from their perspective. Here are a few questions most leads will be asking when they work with an agent that is new to them:

- "How are you going to get me the most money?"
- "How much time is it going to take?"
- "What's your track record?"
- "What's your marketing plan?"
- "Who else is involved in the process/team?"

Share Case Studies, Not Promises

Most agents frame their presentation around all the promises of things that are going to happen in the future. What if you reverse engineered it and made it far more relatable to the customer? Think about this in terms of a case study.

This means you continue your story by sharing case studies of how you have helped customers in similar situations. This allows you to demonstrate your expertise and experience in an engaging and memorable way.

For example:

"When I helped Tom and Kathy sell their three-bedroom, two-bath home down the street, what worked really well was..."

Then you follow that up with more details of your case study. Here are a few things you may want to add to your case study:

- Earned the listing
- Staged the home to take professional photos and video
- Had eighty-three agents at the broker preview
- Major online impressions
- Had eighty-seven people at the mega open house
- Received eight offers

- Sold for 3% over asking price!

Before the Listing Presentation

You want to know a secret about listing presentations? The trust and the momentum start before you even show up! Yes, you should have a killer listing presentation, but here's what you should do before you meet with your customers:

1. Send a video confirmation.

We live in a faceless society, and it is super easy to just send out another email. When you send out a video, it totally changes the dynamic. There are several services out there you can use to send out videos; I like BombBomb.

I'd recommend using a script like this:

> Hey [name],
>
> I'm Tom Ferry from Banana Real Estate. Thank you so much for the opportunity to come out and talk to you about the sale of your home. I know you had a lot of choices in real estate professionals here locally, and I'm honored and thrilled to talk to you about how I can sell your home for top dollar in the shortest amount of time.

Below, you are going to see a number of things that will help you make an informed decision about selecting the right agent for the job of selling your home.

The first thing you are going to see is a link to my "marketing plan." You are also going to see a link to all the transactions we've completed in the last twelve months. It is important that you take a look at that so you can see the number of people we are serving by helping them buy and sell real estate.

You are also going to see what other people are saying about our service levels and the service we provide for our customers.

You'll also see my team of experts, because we've learned that it takes more than one person to market, sell, manage, and close a complex real estate transaction. Because when you choose me, you get all these people working on your behalf!

Finally, you'll get a link to all the paperwork.

I've talked to some agents who are really concerned about the work it would take to create an asset like that. In all honesty, you could film it on your phone pretty quickly. But I think the real concern is the fear of rejection...What if the client decides they don't want to work with you after receiving that message?

Good! That means you didn't have to waste your time and go there and show up in person and make a presentation to find out they didn't want to work with you. Maybe they just were curious about the value of their house or aren't even close to being ready yet.

2. Link to "My Marketing Proposal" and a photo at the board.

As mentioned in the video, you should have a link to your marketing proposal. The average agent has eleven items on their marketing plan list; what if you take yours to thirty to forty and also make it visual? You will stand out from the competition! Take a photo of you and your team standing in front of a board writing out different ideas that you have for this potential client. This shows them that you've already started working on their personal marketing plan.

3. Link to track record/map.

Send a social proof piece of all the homes you've sold, which is easily created using Google Maps. If you're new to real estate, you can always talk about the work your team has done. Just be honest and say that on the map.

4. Link to reviews.

Let other people tell them that you are a rockstar and about the amazing services you and your team provide. Zillow reviews are great for this, but you could also include a link to your testimonials page or even a Yelp page.

5. Keep a photo of your team of experts.

Like we mentioned in the preceding script, you want to drive home the expertise your team will provide the customer. We all know that it takes more than one person to market, sell, manage, and close a complex real estate transaction. Show them that if they pick you, they actually get your whole team working on their behalf. Even if you don't have a team on your payroll, you still have a team... your loan officer, title rep, manager, office support staff, etc. Get them all together for a photo!

6. The morning of your appointment, send another video.

Confirm the appointment once again and make sure that they reviewed all the material in your last email. This helps to create a situation where they know you are the expert and you've already built trust before walking in the door.

Be Successful!

Don't overthink all of this. Just show up prepared, and having set the expectations before you even show up. After that, all you have to do is deliver on what you promised and get the win!

MARKETING FOR THE SUCCESS YOU DESERVE

———

Is your marketing driving the success you deserve? Whether you do all the marketing on your own or work with a team, it is one of the key components for the success of your business.

We've covered a lot in this section, and I want to review a few things before we close. Let's start by thinking about marketing to the following key areas.

Market to Your Database

Your database is one of your most important assets. Make sure that you are sending them weekly or monthly emails. This can be content created by you (or someone on your team) as well as content you curate from other websites.

Additionally, you can send out cards for special occasions. Think of things like birthdays, anniversaries, and other relationship management touch points.

Market to Your Geographic Farm

What are you sending out to your geographic farm? I recommend two to three mailers per month, which can include a few things. This could be your social proof card of the "just listed/just sold" as well as your open houses.

How connected are you to your farm? Do you live in the area, know the local business owners, do your shopping in the area? Being a part of the community is an easy way to build connections and expand your sphere of influence.

If you are just starting out in real estate, you may need to go with a sweat equity approach versus a check equity approach. This means you are knocking on doors, shaking hands, and meeting people in person.

Give it some time, and you'll be able to spend more on your marketing efforts, but there is really something to be said for having that connection with your customers.

One last thing about geographic farms...Be sure to give back. If you are truly serving your community, I recommend giving back in some way. A lot of times this means sponsoring a local team or a post in a local publication, but I know you can be more creative with something that is specific to the community you are serving.

Market on Social

Make sure you are putting videos on social! Like I mentioned earlier, I recommend that you do a weekly show where you create value for your followers. Think of this as a live mention video where you simply talk about how the market is doing and demonstrate that you are the local market expert.

There are a ton of other things you can share on social media too, such as videos from your open house or community events. You can also post relevant articles, pictures, and anything else that will provide value to your customers.

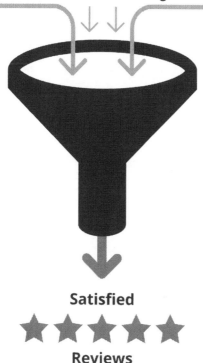

Satisfied

★★★★★

Reviews

Feed the Funnel

There are a ton of ways to get the leads into your funnel, but I want you to take a step back and think about this for a minute...These are real people, who need help. As their agent, you can provide them the solution they are looking for!

You know that if you want to be successful in business, you have to feed that funnel and convert. Every quarter, or at a minimum once per year, you need to adopt some new lead generation sources. You then will test these lead sources out to find out which ones are the best investments. Do this for a minimum of ninety days and keep the lead sources with the highest ROI.

Getting more leads is only half the issue though. You've got to have a system in place to handle those leads! The worst thing you can do is get new leads and watch them slip through the cracks. Make sure that you are creating the right response specific to the channels generated from the leads.

Most importantly, remember to treat your leads the same. Stop judging opportunities and just serve the client!

Know Your Numbers

When it comes to leads, you need to know your numbers.

- Do you know your cost per lead per lead source?
  → The cost to get a new name in your database.

- Cost per appointment per lead source?
  - → Not all of your leads will pick up the phone, and not all of them will meet with you.
- Cost per sale per lead source?
  - → Of all the people you meet with, only a percentage will buy or sell with you.

Follow Up with Your Leads

I've already mentioned it, but you have to follow up with the leads in your funnel. The money is made in the follow-up, and your odds of success are much higher if you can follow up within five minutes.

Remember that just because your leads might not be ready to buy right now, you still need to stay "top of mind" with them. You do this by nurturing your leads until they are ready to make that decision.

FIVE IS YOUR MAGIC NUMBER

So all this information is great, but without action it won't make a difference. If you want to be a top-tier agent that is crushing it, you need to know the magic number, which is five!

Why five? When I surveyed the thousands of agents who are part of my coaching program, I found the number five came up consistently with agents who were dominating their market.

The Power of Five

1. Prospect five-plus hours a week.

Those agents who were most successful prospected for at least five hours per week. Marketing is math, and you know that not every call will convert. But at that volume, it is not a matter of *if* but *when* you start to move those leads forward!

How you get in those five hours is up to you. I've had some of my coaching clients live stream their prospecting calls to my private coaching Facebook groups. They do this for accountability, and I'm so proud of these rockstars! By the way, if you want to learn more about my coaching programs, be sure to visit TomFerry.com for additional information.

The important part is not how many days, but the consistency of your action. You are putting time on your schedule every week to get that five hours in with laserlike focus.

2. Have five or more open houses a month.

How many open houses have you done this month? My survey showed again that the most successful agents had five or more open houses per month. If your open houses are feeling stale or boring, be sure to check out the mega open house method I mentioned earlier in the book.

3. Follow up five or more times on every lead.

This point is critical and I don't want you to miss it...The money is made in the follow-up. There is a reason I keep driving this one home, because you have to do it if you want to be successful! You and I both know you can't just call or message once and never reach out again. The reality is you'll probably need to follow up five or more times! You have to stay top of mind with your leads.

Bottom Line

The bottom line is that through your marketing, you're empowering and informing your audience. By doing this, you are building trust and giving them the information they need to make good decisions.

CONCLUSION

———

So now it's up to you...what ACTIONS will you take to move forward in a positive direction? As you think about your action plan, I'm reminded of some of the more powerful concepts from Jim Collins's book, *Good to Great*:

- Chronic inconsistency is mediocrity.
- You are not entitled to be successful; you are entitled to work harder.
- I'm not failing, I'm growing.
- A "not-to-do" list is just as critical as a "to-do" list.
- Without dates, all you have is a wish list.
- If you have more than three priorities, you have no priorities.

With those thoughts, I'll leave you with this last checklist that has enabled many solo agents to move from their first sale to leading a thriving team.

The Eight-Step Plan for Growth

1. **No Budget and No Leads:** Whether you have money or not, don't let lack of resourcefulness get in your way. I teach a concept called "sweat equity or check equity," so no matter what your financial status, there is a positive path forward.

2. **Diversify Lead Generation and Create a Plan:** Simply put, struggling agents have one or two inconsistent sources of leads, and thriving agents have eight or more consistent sources of leads. Always be testing—based on current market conditions—at least one new way to generate business. Over time, add those sources that work to your business.

3. **Consistency and Conversion:** Consistency is key! Connect and convert by doing your hour of power every morning! The amount of leads isn't the number that matters, it's the amount you are converting. Make conversions a game, and take your business to the next level!

4. **Hire an Assistant:** Wondering when's a good time for you to hire an assistant? Then you probably need one now! Every agent that hires an assistant ends up growing their business substantially. Once you hire

the right assistant and delegate to them the day-to-day tasks, you will be free to focus on your highest and best use of time: planning, lead generation, appointment setting, and negotiating.

5. **Grow Your Team:** Not everyone should have a team, yet we know a team out produces an individual. Understand and know the signs when it's right to join a team or start a team.

6. **Team Out Produces Me:** Good leaders know that they are only as successful as their team. When growing your team, hire the right people and build a machine. Your team should be outproducing you!

7. **Extend the Cash Cow:** Being a cash cow means you have more money than you know what to do with, because you operationalize your business and have it running even when you are out of the office. You do this by planning, working on diversification, consistency, conversion, serving your customers, hiring great people to grow the business, and turning everything into a system.

8. **Exit and Success Plan:** Your business should now have a life of its own. You will now be at the point where you only need to be at the office once or twice a week, or you don't have to go in at all. This is where you have the option of selling your business or turning it over to loved ones. In order to get to this point, you must have the right mindset for success.

Uncomfortable

Did parts of this book make you uncomfortable? If not, I haven't done my job. We both know that growth comes when you get comfortable being uncomfortable. It is really about you pushing out past your comfort zones.

Are you willing to get uncomfortable to reach that next level? I believe in you and know that you are capable of incredible things! I know this because you are the kind of agent that is willing to do the work, serve your customers, and create a better real estate experience for everyone you interact with.

ABOUT THE AUTHOR

TOM FERRY earned the ranking of #1 coach in real estate for four consecutive years by the Swanepoel Power 200 for his charismatic style of coaching and innovative marketing and business strategies. Tom is the author of the #1 *New York Times* bestseller, *Life! By Design*. His widely popular YouTube series, the #TomFerryShow, has benefited countless real estate professionals throughout the world, providing tips and techniques that have proven invaluable for building a successful real estate business.

Be sure to visit
TomFerry.com
for information about our

Success Coaching

Life Changing Events

Training Products

Follow Us On Social!

tomferry   tomferry   tomferry   RealEstateTrainingTF

93781147R00128

Made in the USA
Middletown, DE
16 October 2018